The One

How to Know and Trust God's Sovereign Plan for Your Future Marriage

By Mark Ballenger

Copyright © 2018 by Mark Ballenger

All rights reserved. No part of this publication may be reproduced, distributed, or transmitted in any form or by any means, including photocopying, recording, or other electronic or mechanical methods, without the prior written permission of the publisher, except in the case of brief quotations embodied in critical reviews and certain other noncommercial uses permitted by copyright law.

For blogs, free eBooks, and more resources by Mark Ballenger, please visit ApplyGodsWord.com.

Contact us at:
Website: ApplyGodsWord.com
YouTube: www.youtube.com/c/ApplyGodsWordcomMarkBallenger
Twitter: @Apply_GodsWord
Facebook: www.facebook.com/ApplyGodsWord/
Email: markballenger@applygodsword.com

Book Cover Attribution:
The book cover was designed by Mark Ballenger. The pictures for the book cover were found on https://pixabay.com/. Images on Pixabay are released under Creative Commons CC0. The source information to these pictures is provided to give credit to their authors who have graciously posted them on Pixabay to be used for free by others.

Front cover top: https://pixabay.com/en/girl-smiling-1996989/ by greekfood-tamystika
https://pixabay.com/en/users/greekfood-tamystika-2743349/

Front cover bottom: https://pixabay.com/en/people-man-guy-headset-beard-2583061/ by StockSnap
https://pixabay.com/en/users/StockSnap-894430/

Back cover bottom: https://pixabay.com/en/folk-male-portrait-son-in-law-3135119/ by Ertan Bayraktar
https://pixabay.com/en/users/ErtanBayraktar-7952799/

Back cover top: https://pixabay.com/en/wedding-dresses-castle-bride-1486005/ by maya_7966
https://pixabay.com/en/users/maya_7966-1170035/

Unless otherwise noted, all Scripture references are from the ESV.

About the Author

Mark Ballenger is a blogger, vlogger, and online Bible teacher. He is the founder of the popular AGW Ministries (Apply God's Word Ministries). Through ApplyGodsWord.com, his YouTube channel, and his other social media outlets, Mark's teachings have been seen by millions.

His writings have also been featured on a variety of popular online ministries including DesiringGod.org, RelevantMagazing.com, ChurchLeaders.com, Beliefnet.com, and many more.

Mark has served in a variety of ministry roles over the years. He has served as a pastor where he primarily worked with 18 to 35-year-olds. He has worked at a Christian men's crisis center where he served men of all ages dealing with homelessness, mental illness, and addictions. He has also served as a missionary in West Africa. Mark has a master's degree in pastoral counseling from Liberty Baptist Theological Seminary.

Mark met his wife Bethany while serving as a missionary in West Africa. They were married in 2008 and currently have two children. They live in Cleveland, Ohio.

If you would like to stay up to date with all of Mark's newest content, you can join the thousands of others on his email list. When you join this list you also get instant access to a variety of free eBooks by Mark including *The Ultimate Guide to Christian Singleness*. You can join this list by simply visiting ApplyGodsWord.com.

Table of Contents

Introduction: God Is Trustworthy 6

Chapter 1: Is There Such a Thing as "The One"? 10

Chapter 2: Does God's Will Always Happen in Relationships? 22

Chapter 3: How Does God's Sovereignty and Man's Responsibility Work Together in Relationships? 33

Chapter 4: Does Your Sin and Satan's Temptation Cancel Out God's Sovereign Plan for Your Future Marriage? 42

Chapter 5: Why Pray About Your Future Marriage in Your Singleness If God Is Sovereign? 56

Chapter 6: Why Is God Waiting to Show You the Date He Has Set for Your Wedding Day? 66

Chapter 7: How Will God Reveal The One to You? (Part 1: Through His Word) 79

Chapter 8: How Will God Reveal The One to You? (Part 2: Through His Spirit) 91

Chapter 9: How Will God Reveal The One to You? (Part 3: Through Your Circumstances) 102

Chapter 10: What Should You Do If You Are Not Sure If God Is Revealing The One to You? 115

Chapter 11: Does God Ever Speak Through Dreams and "Prophetic Words" About Relationships? 125

Chapter 12: How Can You Overcome the Fear of the Unknowns and Move Forward Towards Your Future Marriage? 137

Thank You! 149

Appendix 150

Introduction
God Is Trustworthy

What is God's plan for your singleness, dating, and marriage? Well . . . I have no idea.

If you haven't closed the book already, let me explain what I do know and what I hope to teach you. I don't know the specifics of God's plan for you and your relationships. I don't know if you will be single forever or if you will be married next year. I do know, however, that God does have a plan for you. I know this because I believe the Bible, and the Bible says God loves you, is guiding you, and has a good plan for your life. When we put our faith in Jesus and follow God, we will experience his goodness:

> "In him we were also chosen, having been predestined according to the plan of him who works out everything in conformity with the purpose of his will." (Ephesians 1:11)

> "For I know the plans I have for you," declares the Lord, "plans to prosper you and not to harm you, plans to give you hope and a future." (Jeremiah 29:11)

> "Your eyes saw my unformed body; all the days ordained for me were written in your book before one of them came to be." (Psalm 139:16)

> "The Lord will fulfill his purpose for me; your steadfast love, O Lord, endures forever. Do not forsake the work of your hands." (Psalm 138:8)

> "And we know that for those who love God all things work together for good, for those who are called according to his purpose." (Romans 8:28)

In other words, God is sovereign. The rest of this book is meant to explain that truth in the context of relationships. He really is in control of the details of your life, and this applies to your singleness, dating, and future marriage as well. He has planned who you will meet, when you will meet him or her, and what the outcome of that meeting will be. He knows who you will marry and who you won't marry.

Why write a whole book on this? Because the above statements cause so many questions for Christian singles. Often people start feeling like a robot and as though their choices don't matter when they hear that God is sovereign. While the Bible completely affirms God's total control of everything, it also affirms that God allows our human choices to really matter.

My goal is not only to try to explain all this in the best way I can, but my deeper hope is that in learning about God's power and sovereign plan for your relationships, you will grow to trust and obey him more. As we will discuss throughout this book, the biblical response to God's sovereignty is not to feel like a robot and obey him less because you think your choices don't matter. When you properly understand God's power this will cause you to trust

God more, obey him more, and make the best choices you can as you use your free will to follow God's plan for you.

This is not a step-by-step plan on how to thrive in singleness, dating, and marriage. You can visit my website, ApplyGodsWord.com, to find that type of information. I'm a big believer in applying the Bible to our lives in practical ways. But that's not my goal in this book. This book has a much narrower focus. I want to help you see that God does have a plan for you, which means you do not need to be anxious and you can trust him. Lastly, I want to teach you how you can know God's plan and hear God's voice when it comes to making decisions in relationships. I want to show you how God will reveal "the one" to you when the right time comes.

Throughout this book I'm going to be talking about your "future marriage." As I've already confessed, I'm not a fortune teller so I don't actually know if God does have a marriage planned for you. Most Christians are called to marriage, some are called to singleness. So in this book I'm just going to be assuming God does have a marriage in your future so I can help you trust God to bring his plan into fruition for you.

However, in the appendix of this book I have included some other resources about how to know if God is calling you to singleness. You may benefit from reading those resources if you have questions about your call to singleness or marriage. I also have another book I give away for free (as an eBook) on my website called *The Ultimate Guide to Christian Singleness*. (It's also available in paperback if you prefer turning physical pages like me.) If you want to thrive in singleness, use your singleness, and learn more about what the Bible says regarding Christian singleness, that book may really benefit you.

I hope the pages ahead embolden your trust in God and in his ability to bring you to "the one" he has planned for you to marry.

Chapter 1
Is There Such a Thing as "The One"?

Do I believe God has a specific person for you to marry (if you are called to marriage)? Yes. Why do I believe that? Because I believe God is sovereign and really does have plans for each of our lives.

The reason there is debate amongst Christians on whether or not there is such a thing as "the one" is because the Bible doesn't flat out say one way or the other. To me, asking this question about whether or not God predetermines who you will marry is a theological question regarding God's sovereignty and man's free will more than it is a relationship question.

Those who emphasize God's will over man's freewill say God has predetermined who you will marry because God has predetermined everything. Those who emphasize man's free will over God's sovereign will say that anyone can marry anyone and God has nothing to do with who you actually marry one day.

What I say is that we should not emphasize God's will over man's free will or vice versa because these two biblical truths are not opposed to one another at all. Yes, God has planned who you will marry. And yes, you will choose your spouse. Now let's really start unpacking what the Bible says.

God Is In Control of Who You Will Marry Because God Is In Control of Everything

Throughout the pages of Scripture, you will see verse and verse proclaiming the omnipotence (all-powerfulness) of God. According to Scripture, everything that happens is in accordance with God's sovereign will.

In the next chapter we will discuss why things like sin, divorce, and hurts in relationships occur if God is omnibenevolent (all-good) and omnipotent, but for now we just want to establish what the Bible actually says about God's power to plan everything and accomplish everything that he plans.

> "In him we have obtained an inheritance, having been predestined according to the purpose of him who works all things according to the counsel of his will, [12] so that we who were the first to hope in Christ might be to the praise of his glory." (Ephesians 1:11-12)
>
> "Our God is in the heavens; he does all that he pleases." (Psalm 115:3)
>
> "I know that you can do all things, and that no purpose of yours can be thwarted." (Job 42:2)
>
> "The Lord has established his throne in the heavens, and his kingdom rules over all." (Psalm 103:19)

"The Lord of hosts has sworn: 'As I have planned, so shall it be, and as I have purposed, so shall it stand.'" (Isaiah 14:24)

"For the Lord of hosts has purposed, and who will annul it? His hand is stretched out, and who will turn it back?" (Isaiah 14:27)

"The lot is cast into the lap, but its every decision is from the Lord." (Proverbs 16:33)

"So then he has mercy on whomever he wills, and he hardens whomever he wills." (Romans 9:18)

"Whatever the Lord pleases, he does, in heaven and on earth, in the seas and all deeps." (Psalm 135:6)

"Who has spoken and it came to pass, unless the Lord has commanded it?" (Lamentations 3:37)

"The Lord has made everything for its purpose, even the wicked for the day of trouble." (Proverbs 16:4)

"Is a trumpet blown in a city, and the people are not afraid? Does disaster come to a city, unless the Lord has done it?" (Amos 3:6)

"See now that I, even I, am he, and there is no god beside me; I kill and I make alive; I wound and I heal; and there is none that can deliver out of my hand." (Deuteronomy 32:39)

"As for you, you meant evil against me, but God meant it for good, to bring it about that many people should be kept alive, as they are today." (Genesis 50:20)

"I form light and create darkness, I make well-being and create calamity, I am the Lord, who does all these things." (Isaiah 45:7)

"I make known the end from the beginning, from ancient times, what is still to come. I say, 'My purpose will stand, and I will do all that I please.'" (Isaiah 46:10, NIV)

"For we are his workmanship, created in Christ Jesus for good works, which God prepared beforehand, that we should walk in them." (Ephesians 2:10)

"The heart of man plans his way, but
the Lord establishes his steps." (Proverbs 16:9)

Obviously none of these Bible verses say, "Yes, there is such a thing as the one. God has planned who you will marry." However, if you can't see the implication of these verses regarding relationships, there's not much more I can do to convince you.

When we read the Bible, it is clear that God is sovereign and in complete control of everything. If we accept this truth, then we must also accept that God does actually have a plan that he will accomplish regarding who you will marry because God has a plan that he will accomplish for everything.

God Chooses The One for You, And You Choose Your Own Husband or Wife

I'm not here to solve a debate that has been going on for centuries about God's sovereignty and man's free will. What I firmly believe, however, is that God is sovereign, and in his sovereignty he is able to bring about his ordained will through the free choices of human beings.

You are not a robot. Your choices really do matter and have consequences. And God is still sovereign and will bring about the ends that he has predestined to occur from the beginning. The Bible verses that prove this point perhaps most clearly are in Acts 2:22-23:

> "Men of Israel, hear these words: Jesus of Nazareth, a man attested to you by God with mighty works and wonders and signs that God did through him in your midst, as you yourselves know— ^{23} this Jesus, delivered up according to the definite plan and foreknowledge of God, you crucified and killed by the hands of lawless men."

Who crucified Jesus? Lawless men. Who planned for the crucifixion to happen before humanity even began? God. People chose to kill Jesus and through their choices God produced his sovereign plan which he had predestined before time began. Many people limit the topic of foreordination simply to salvation, but as John Piper states in his article, *Does God Control All Things All the Times?*:

> "God works *all things* according to his will. Here's Ephesians 1:11: "In him we have obtained an

inheritance, having been predestined according to the purpose of him who works all things according to the counsel of his will." Let me say it again. He works all things according to the counsel of his will. . . . that means he always controls everything."

When you read through Ephesians 1:3-6, for example, it is clear that before the world began God chose people to be redeemed through the gospel, " . . . he chose us in him [Christ] before the foundation of the world, that we should be holy and blameless before him. In love he predestined us for adoption to himself as sons through Jesus Christ, according to the purpose of his will . . . ." If God predestined us to be redeemed in Christ from our sin, does this mean God caused sin? Nope (James 1:13-15, Hebrews 6:18). But through the sinfulness of man God brought about his sovereign will to redeem man through the gospel.

Again, I know my explanation here is not going to put a little bow on this debate and make Arminians and Calvinists sing Kumbaya together. My point is that God does have a sovereign will and that truth does not contradict the other truth that each person is alive and free to obey and disobey God in the life he or she lives. With all this in mind, here is the best way I have come to understand the relationship between God's sovereignty and man's choices: God brings about his sovereign will through the free choices of human beings.

God is greater than a micro-manager god who needs to control people to get the outcomes he wants. He is greater than a passive god who simply sits back and responds to humans as they run the show. God in his greatness is able to create free agents while also being in control of the details to the story he is writing through their hands.

What Does the Bible Say About The One?

Again, as I said earlier, the Bible doesn't plainly say "God has a special person just for you to marry," or "God chooses who you marry." So to get the most biblical answer to this question about whether or not there is "the one," I believe you must consistently apply your best understanding of biblical doctrine. Take the general truths in Scripture and apply them to this question about "the one." Therefore I think you will get different answers from people depending upon their theological perspective.

If you are asking me if *I* think there is "the one" (for those who are called to marriage and not singleness), I would say "yes" because I believe God has a plan for everything. I believe God planned for me to be with my wife and not another woman. I believe Psalm 139:16, " . . . all the days ordained for me were written in your book before one of them came to be." While God has ordained my days, I still need to go out and live them through my own choices. And yet if God plans something, it happens.

So my best articulation of the whole thing, again, is this: God is sovereign, and in his sovereignty he is able to bring about his ordained will through the free choices of human beings. Therefore if I apply that belief to this topic of "the one," I would say: God has one specific person for you to marry, and he will bring about this marriage through your personal, un-manipulated choices.

My point is that God is sovereign and man is free to make real choices. I choose not to violate either of these biblical truths. As Charles Spurgeon famously put it when asked about how he reconciles the *apparent* tension in the Bible between God's sovereignty and man's free will, "I was once asked to reconcile these two statements, and I answered, 'No, I never reconciled friends.'"

So does God have someone specific in mind just for you (if you are called to marriage)? Yes. Is it your choice to marry who you want to marry and will your choice have good and bad consequences? Yes.

Here's What I Do Mean and Don't Mean When I Say "The One"

To be clear, I'm using the phrase "the one" to mean a specific person God has planned for you to marry. I mean this in contrast to the opposing idea that God doesn't have a plan for your marriage and is simply waiting for you to tell him who it is that will be your spouse. I want to be clear by what I mean by "the one" because there are many things people often associate with this phrase which I do not mean.

Some people ask, "Is there one person for everyone according to the Bible?" If the question was asked this way and I was being extra literal that day, I would say "no." For starters, not everyone is called to marriage, therefore not everyone will have a "soulmate" so to speak. Also there are specific circumstances where God condones remarriage thus someone could have had more than "one" person they were married to when it's all said and done. When deaths occur, for example, remarriage is God's plan for some. Therefore by "the one" I don't literally mean that God wants every human being to be married to just one human being in their lifetime.

I also understand why people adamantly counsel young adults that there is not "the one" out there. I disagree theologically, but I understand the motivation in cautioning people to not look for "the one." I think the danger in looking for your soulmate is that you end up looking for a perfect person you created in your head rather than being more practical and biblical about the whole process. And I totally agree and have written a lot in other places about how perfectionism is detrimental to actually getting married to someone.

I also agree that the thought of there just being "one person God wants me to marry" can create a lot of pressure and fear causing people, especially young adults, to ask the counter question, "Well if there is just one specific person God wants me to marry, what happens if I marry the wrong person? Will our lives be miserable?" I believe compatibility in relationships is not the primary variable in the equation of marital happiness. Meeting "the one" is not you entering the marital "promise land" of bliss. When you meet "the one," I just mean you have met the specific person God wants you to marry. I don't mean this person will be exactly like the person you dreamed about and will be the perfect fit for you. There is not a perfect fit out there.

When I say "the one," I don't mean this is the person who will always make you happy and if you are unhappy they must not be the one. I'm not saying God has one person meant to fill you perfectly. Only Jesus is the true One in that sense. So I agree that thinking there is "the one" will cause people to question later in marriage, "I wonder if I married the wrong person?" But this is due to poor overall theology and immaturity and is not a reason to now say God doesn't have an actual plan for your life.

Why This Common Argument Found Among Christians Does Not Disprove "The One"

Some people use an argument that goes like this to debunk the idea that there is just one person God wants you to marry:

> "Well, if there really is "the one" for each person God has destined you to marry, what if someone married the wrong "one"? This would set off a cosmic chain of events inevitably ruining tons of other matches."

While this argument is cute, I don't think it really holds much weight when talking about the sovereignty of God. If the premise is that God has a will for people and when they don't follow it they have forever ruined God's will, thus this is evidence God does not have a sovereign will because God would never do that, to me this is illogical and unbiblical.

This argument is built on a false premise that God can have a sovereign will and yet man can break it. Theologically, however, God's sovereign will is accomplished every time because God is sovereign. If God's sovereign will could be broken it would not be a sovereign will. Therefore if God has picked a specific person for you in his sovereignty, it would be impossible for you to not marry that person, thus the argument of a cosmic mismatch catastrophe is nonsense.

If you as a Christian hold the same beliefs as me about God's sovereignty and believe God has a plan for everything (Jeremiah 29:11 , Proverbs 16:9, Jeremiah 29:11-14, Proverbs 19:21, Jeremiah 1:5, Jeremiah 10:23, James 4:13-15), to be consistent you must also believe God has a specific plan for who you will marry.

Reflection Questions:

1. Do you believe God is sovereign? Why or why not?

2. Pick one Bible verse that stuck out to you from this chapter. What did you learn from this verse?

3. Do you believe there is one "soulmate" for each person and if one person marries the wrong one it will set off a chain reaction of people not marrying their soulmate? Why or why not?

4. How do you feel when you hear "God is sovereign"? Does it make you feel less free or freer? What questions does this phrase cause you to have?

5. Read Acts 2:22-23. What do you learn from this passage?

Chapter 2
Does God's Will Always Happen in Relationships?

Does God's will always prevail? More specifically, does God's will always happen in relationships? This is a common question for Christians when it comes to dating and marriage.

When we talk about the will of God, it can be confusing because we know God is omnibenevolent (all good) and omnipotent (all powerful/sovereign) and yet bad things happen in life and relationships. So why do bad things happen if God has all the power and desires good for humans?

Sadly Christians often feel torn to choose between the all-powerful God or the all-loving God. They usually choose the all-loving God and thus assume God's will does not always happen. But we do not need to choose between God's power and God's goodness. We need to increase our understanding of how they work together.

We often make the jump that God's will must not always happen because sinful, bad things happen all the time. Since God would never plan for evil or cause sin, God's will must not always prevail. But there are so many Bible verses that talk about God's predetermined will always happening. So which is it? Does God's will always happen in relationships or not?

The key to answering questions like these is to realize there are two types of "God's will" in the Bible. In this chapter I will explain God's sovereign will, his prescribed will, and then how these two "wills" play out in Christian relationships.

God's Sovereign Will Always Happens in Relationships

The first "will of God" is what many, including myself, refer to as God's sovereign will. When we say that God is sovereign, we mean that he has a plan and always accomplishes that plan. Sovereignty is a prerequisite for divinity. If you can't do what you want whenever you want, you are not God.

Over and over again the Bible teaches us that God is completely in control of every molecule that has ever existed. What happens in reality is always God's will because God is always in complete control of reality. Otherwise you are saying God is not in control and the causes that form our reality are more powerful than God. Yes, we live in a cause and effect world, but the Bible teaches us that the outcomes are already determined through God's power (Matthew 26:39, Matthew 10:29, Acts 4:27–28, Daniel 4:35).

> "In him we have obtained an inheritance, having been predestined according to the purpose of him who works all things according to the counsel of his will." (Ephesians 1:11)

> "The lot is cast into the lap, but its every decision is from the Lord." (Proverbs 16:33)

So God's sovereign will always happens in relationships. God's will, in this sense, always happens no matter what.

But there are many things that displease God that occur on earth. So how do we reconcile God's sovereignty with his displeasure towards pain, sin, and hurt in the lives of humans?

God's Prescribed Will Does Not Always Happen in Relationships

The second type of "will of God" which the Bible teaches us about is what I refer to as God's prescribed will. I like the word "prescribed" because this type of "will" is God's directions and instructions to us. Like a prescription from the doctor, God has prescribed a way of life for us and given us commands we should follow. Others have referred to this as "God's will of command." This type of "will of God" is what God wants and has told humans to do but which he gives us the option to fulfill or not fulfill. It is God's will that you obey him, but we all know we do not always obey.

> "But the Pharisees and the lawyers rejected the purpose of God for themselves, not having been baptized by him." (Luke 7:30)

> "Not everyone who says to me, 'Lord, Lord,' will enter the kingdom of heaven, but the one who does the will of my Father who is in heaven." (Matthew 7:21)

> "For this is the will of God, your sanctification: that you abstain from sexual immorality." (1 Thessalonians 4:3)

> " . . . give thanks in all circumstances; for this is the will of God in Christ Jesus for you." (1 Thessalonians 5:18)

> "And the world is passing away along with its desires, but whoever does the will of God abides forever." (1 John 2:17)

Here we can see that humans often break God's will for their life and do not follow God's plan. The Pharisees "rejected the purpose of God for themselves" because they did not obey God truly. When we sin and disobey, God's will is not done.

People become angry or confused when they think of all the devastation on the earth and then they hear someone like me say "God's will always happens." The problem is that they are pitting God's sovereign will and his prescribed will against one another. God does not cause evil things to occur in our relationships, but he does have control over the evil things that happen.

God's Sovereign Will Still Prevails Even When Humans Do Not Follow God's Will for Their Life

When you take God's sovereign will and God's prescribed will both into account, you can begin to see how God is in control even of things that he does not want. As John Piper puts it in his article *What Is the Will of God and How Do We Know It?*:

> "In fact, knowing the difference between these two meanings of "the will of God" is crucial to

understanding one of the biggest and most perplexing things in all the Bible, namely, that God is sovereign over all things and yet disapproves of many things. Which means that God disapproves of some of what he ordains to happen. That is, he forbids some of the things he brings about. And he commands some of the things he hinders. Or to put it most paradoxically: God wills some events in one sense that he does not will in another sense."

No matter what happens in life, God is in control. Even when Satan acts, God is the one who allows it (Luke 22:31, Job 1:6-12). When humans do evil things, God allows it. God either causes or allows everything that happens. Therefore God is in control.

But God gave us commands for a reason. The Bible tells us what ought to be. God wants good for humans which is why he tells us how to live our lives; but to allow us true freedom so we can experience true love, he allows us to disobey him. We are not breaking his sovereign will, but we are breaking his prescribed will for us. Again, I refer to Piper who states:

> "Here's an example from 1 Peter. In 1 Peter 3:17 Peter writes, "It is better to suffer for doing good, *if that should be God's will*, than for doing evil." In other words, *it may be God's will that Christians suffer for doing good*. He has in mind persecution. But persecution of Christians who do not deserve it is sin. So again, God sometimes wills that events come about that include sin. 'It is better to suffer for doing good, if that should be God's will.'"

Our sin does not mean God is not in control. Evil does not mean God is not in control. It means God allows sin and allows evil. You can break God's commands, but you cannot break God's authority over you. Whether you obey him or not, God is still the Master of the universe.

The Comfort that Comes From the Confusion

If it feels like I am straining to find the words to explain how God works, it's because I am. If I wasn't straining and pushing our minds past the brink of complete human understanding, I would be worried. If you ever think you know God so well that there is no more mystery to him, that there are no more questions, that he fits neatly into your worldview, then odds are you are limiting who God really is. If you don't have questions about God you don't know the true God. Isaiah 55:6-9 explains:

> "Seek the Lord while he may be found; call upon him while he is near; [7] let the wicked forsake his way, and the unrighteous man his thoughts; let him return to the Lord, that he may have compassion on him, and to our God, for he will abundantly pardon. [8] For my thoughts are not your thoughts, neither are your ways my ways, declares the Lord. [9] For as the heavens are higher than the earth, so are my ways higher than your ways and my thoughts than your thoughts."

Notice how this passage starts, "Seek the Lord while he may be found; call upon him while he is near." Why? "For my thoughts are not your thoughts, neither are your ways my ways. For as the heavens are higher than the earth, so are my ways higher than your ways and my thoughts than your thoughts." Our inability to fully grasp God's power is not a reason to doubt him, it is a reason to believe in him and seek him.

I would be concerned if I thought my understanding of God was total and complete because that would be a sign I created my ideas about this god in my head. The created never have full comprehension of their Creator. The fact that God can bring about his sovereign will even though he has given us a prescribed will to obey and disobey is ultimately beyond me. I understand it generally. I understand what the Bible says. I understand how I am to apply these truths. But I do not understand how God accomplishes all this.

Pride gets mad about this lack of complete comprehension about God and causes the human heart to turn away from him. Humility is relieved that God is greater than us and causes the human heart to trust God even more. When we know God is greater, it should embolden our belief in God and not diminish it. While God has certainly made himself known, approachable in Christ, and comprehensible to some degree, the Bible does not claim man will be able to understand him fully and wholly. In Christ we can know God, be fully united with him, and actually communicate with him, but full comprehension of his essence is not a part of the promise.

> "Oh, the depth of the riches and wisdom and knowledge of God! How unsearchable are his judgments and how inscrutable his ways! 'For who has known the mind of the Lord, or who has been his

> counselor?' 'Or who has given a gift to him that he might be repaid?' For from him and through him and to him are all things. To him be glory forever. Amen." (Romans 11:33-36)

It is right for every Christian to pursue the knowledge of God, fully expecting to attain it. God has revealed himself to us. He has given us a written record of his truths and sent his Son to earth for this very purpose. But we must also recognize that as human beings, if we were to fully comprehend God, it would go against what God has said, thus disproving that the God described in the Bible is the true God.

Does God's Will Always Happen in Relationships?

So now let's apply what we've learned to relationships.

God's prescribed will does not always happen in relationships. His sovereign will, however, does always happen in relationships. He does not want bad things to happen, but even the bad things that do happen are under God's control. Everything that happens is either directly caused by God or allowed by God, and everything that exists in reality exists because God has allowed it to exist that way.

These same theological truths should be applied when answering, "Does God's will always happen in a relationship?" It depends on what "will" you are referring to. God does not will that evil, abuse, adultery, or any sin ever happen in a relationship. But God is in control of your life even when these things do happen. He knows what will happen and why it happened and how he will gain glory through it all.

Many times people want to know if God's will always happens in relationships because they want to know if they can miss out on something good in relationships that God wanted for them. The answer to that is yes. Anytime you sin you are missing out on something good God has for you.

However, we can take this too far and start assuming that even when we are obeying God's word we will miss God's will. This is impossible. If you do your best to obey God's will of command, that's all you can do. The rest is in God's control. You are required to obey God's prescribed will through his grace, through being filled with the Spirit, and as you are being sanctified. God is responsible for his sovereign will.

Cut through all the confusion that arises in relationships by doing your best to apply the word of God to your relationships. That's God's will for you. Love God and love people. Don't worry about what God does or does not have planned for you in specific ways in relationships. We don't know if he plans for you to be with that person or this person, to be married this year or never.

What we do know is that he has good planned for you. When you obey God's word you will experience God's goodness.

> "But be doers of the word, and not hearers only, deceiving yourselves. [23] For if anyone is a hearer of the word and not a doer, he is like a man who looks intently at his natural face in a mirror. [24] For he looks

at himself and goes away and at once forgets what he was like. ²⁵ But the one who looks into the perfect law, the law of liberty, and perseveres, being no hearer who forgets but a doer who acts, he will be blessed in his doing." (James 1:22-25)

Reflection Questions:

1. In your own words, explain the difference between God's sovereign will and God's prescribed will.

2. Why do bad things happen in relationships?

3. When you cannot fully comprehend God, what is the most biblical response?

4. How would you answer if someone asked you, "Does God's will always happen in human relationships?"

5. Did you learn anything new from this chapter? If so, what was it? If not, what are your general thoughts about the content in this chapter?

Chapter 3
How Does God's Sovereignty and Man's Responsibility Work Together in Relationships?

All advice about any subject is always rooted in deeper core beliefs. The same is true with Christian dating advice.

Basically there are two camps when it comes to relationship advice found within the church. There are those who say something like, "Just wait for the Lord to bring your spouse. He will bring that person to you at just the right time. It's all in his plan." And then there are those who say something like, "God helps those who help themselves. Get off your butt and start online dating. Actually, my cousin Vinnie is single. You want me to hook you two up?"

If you were to dig deeper into why people advise the way they do when it comes to relationships, you would see that it all stems back to their belief on God's sovereignty and man's free will. Those who emphasize God's sovereign plan will usually tell you to sit back and wait. Those who emphasize man's free will are quicker to tell you to get moving if you want to be married. The flaw in both cases is when we emphasize these truths as contradicting truths rather than just different coexisting truths.

As we've been noting, man's responsibility and God's sovereignty are often seen as opponents. But within the Bible, these two go hand in hand. The Bible does not try to explain how these two can coexist without violating one another. The Bible simply explains how man's responsibility is directly tied to God's sovereignty.

When we substitute one truth for the other, our perspective gets all out of whack and it affects everything, including our beliefs about what we are responsible for and not responsible for in our pursuit of meeting and marrying the one.

Just Because God Is Sovereign Does Not Mean Man Is Free from Responsibility

The wrong response to believing in God's sovereignty is to sit back and do nothing. For example, as John 15:4-8 states:

> "Abide in me, and I in you. As the branch cannot bear fruit by itself, unless it abides in the vine, neither can you, unless you abide in me. [5] I am the vine; you are the branches. Whoever abides in me and I in him, he it is that bears much fruit, for apart from me you can do nothing. [6] If anyone does not abide in me he is thrown away like a branch and withers; and the branches are gathered, thrown into the fire, and burned. [7] If you abide in me, and my words abide in you, ask whatever you wish, and it will be done for you. [8] By this my Father is glorified, that you bear much fruit and so prove to be my disciples."

The fact that we can do nothing good without Christ does not mean we are called to do nothing. Christ gives us power to act, but we must still choose to live in that power and act. Just because God is in control of your future marriage and how you will meet the one is not an excuse to stop following him while you sit back and wait for God to move on your behalf. Yes, all good is because of God. And yes, there is a time to wait on the Lord. But God also expects us to reach out and grab the good he is putting in front of us. There's a time to wait and a time to pursue.

Jesus had to die on the cross for us, but he still tells us to take up our cross daily to deny ourselves (Matthew 16:24). This is an active command, requiring a choice of the will and action from the body. We won't be able to do it if we are not relying on Christ, but we are called to "do" these things with Christ nonetheless. His power makes possible our right choices and actions, but we are still responsible to make these right choices and actions. His power is the reason we have no excuse for not doing good; the fact that he is the only sovereign power able to cause us to do good is not an excuse for our personal failures.

> "Therefore, my beloved, as you have always obeyed, so now, not only as in my presence but much more in my absence, work out your own salvation with fear and trembling, [13] for it is God who works in you, both to will and to work for his good pleasure."
> (Philippians 2:12-13)

If you were to read Philippians 2:13 in isolation, you would have a desire to argue that if it is God who sovereignly works in us to give us both the desire and the power to obey him, then why are we responsible when we disobey God? However, when you read Philippians 2:12 and 13 together, this logic is turned on its head. God's power in us is the reason we should act rightly. His power in us is not an excuse to not act rightly. We are told to obey God. Why? "For it is God who works in you . . . ." God's power in us is why God now expects us to obey him.

God's Sovereignty Is Not Just a Doctrine to Be Understood, It Is Power to Be Relied Upon in Relationships

So if we take this general truth about obeying God through his power and apply it to how Christians should approach dating and getting married, we can see that God's power and plan is not an excuse to sit idly but it is rather the reason we can walk in faith as we seek to do what God wants us to do to receive the things he wants us to receive. Ephesians 2:8-9 have become favorite verses of the modern evangelist, "For by grace you have been saved through faith. And this is not your own doing; it is the gift of God, not a result of works, so that no one may boast."

There should of course be an emphasis that we are saved by grace alone. But grace is not alone, for it is always accompanied by good works by those who truly receive grace. Ephesians 2:8-9 states we are saved by grace through faith, but it is a crime to not read Ephesians 2:10 to emphasize the whole picture Scripture seeks to paint, "For we are his workmanship, created in Christ Jesus for good works, which God prepared beforehand, that we should walk in them." We are not saved by works, but we are saved for good works done unto God.

The Bible points out our desperate need for God's power not to give us an excuse "since it all depends on him anyway." The Bible tells us to rely on God's power so we know there is now no excuse left not to obey him. While these deep truths are given to us in Scripture to show the relationship between salvation (by grace) and the evidence of salvation (good works), the principles apply to how we should approach relationships too.

If you are relying on God's power to bring you and your future spouse together, this will not cause you to be frozen as you do nothing. This will cause you to make the right decisions at the right time as you actually follow God in your life. God's sovereignty and the Christian's responsibility are not opposed. We can live well for Christ because we know God will accomplish his will. Our belief in God's power causes us to step out in faith even more, not less.

When we think about what we don't have in the present, it can seem impossible to imagine how God might provide for us in the future. But our God has raised us from the dead with Christ. He saved you by grace. Therefore your future marriage and how you will meet the one God has for you is not a difficult task compared to what he already has accomplished for you in the gospel.

In Mark 16 the women are going to take care of Jesus' dead body. They don't know who will roll the stone away, "And they were saying to one another, 'Who will roll away the stone for us from the entrance of the tomb?'" (Mark 16:3). But they start walking to the tomb anyway.

In the same way, meeting the one might seem like a giant stone that is impossible to move. We know that God must produce our marriages for us because we know we cannot do it on our own. While we know we need God to produce this miracle, this does not mean God does not want us to start moving forward even when we don't know how it will all come together. Mark 16:1-4 states:

> "When the Sabbath was past, Mary Magdalene, Mary the mother of James, and Salome bought spices, so that they might go and anoint him. ² And very early on the first day of the week, when the sun had risen, they went to the tomb. ³ And they were saying to one another, 'Who will roll away the stone for us from the entrance of the tomb?' ⁴ And looking up, they saw that the stone had been rolled back—it was very large."

The stone blocking the entrance to the tomb was impossible to move. The women could not force themselves to Jesus. Someone had to move the stone for them. And yet they started walking there anyway.

May we be like those women who went to the tomb, knowing the stone was too heavy, but believing nonetheless that God would move it for them somehow. Your focus must not be on the weight of the stones blocking your wedding day; rather your focus must be on the strength of your God to do the impossible.

Bringing you and your future spouse together is not the most impossible thing God will ever do for you. He raised Jesus from the dead and transformed your heart through the gospel if you have put your faith in Jesus. If he can do that, he can do anything.

Don't Get Stuck Thinking About God's Sovereignty. Live With Confidence As You Trust God's Sovereignty

Christian can sometimes have a great understanding of trusting the sovereignty of God but then they can be very immature in their application of this doctrine. God's power is not a reason to do nothing. God's power is the reason we can step out in faith and follow him as he leads us to actually make decisions in our pursuit of good things, like marriage.

If we are telling all the Christian singles to "just" wait, we are creating a flawed system. If everyone is praying and trusting God but doing nothing to actively engage the opposite sex, is it any wonder why so many Christians remain single? If no one is being active then it's no surprise there are so many people sitting at home alone when they wish they were not.

Of course you should be relying on God to bless your search for a spouse. But when you equate "God has a plan for my marriage" with "God will require nothing of me to accomplish his plan for me," you are not thinking biblically. If you believe the only way God will bring about your future marriage union is by you "just waiting" and relying on the actions of "someone out there" to see you, like you, pursue you, get to know you, ask you out, date you, then make you fully comfortable that they want to marry you, then you are setting yourself up for a long wait.

Is God going to accomplish whatever he wants to accomplish? You bet! But nowhere in Scripture does this give humans a free pass on participating. Our job as

Christians is to learn to rely on God's sovereign strength so we can fulfill our human responsibilities better and better every day. "Because God is in control" should cause us to work harder than ever, trusting the whole time that although we are called to act and obey his prescribed will, God is the universal decision maker and his ultimate purpose for our lives is going to be accomplished according to his sovereign will.

Reflection Questions:

1. Before reading this chapter, what was your understanding about the relationship between God's sovereignty and man's responsibility? Has anything changed after reading this chapter? Explain.

2. Study Philippians 2:12-13. Why should we work out our salvation with fear and trembling?

3. What can you learn from the women in Mark 16 who did not know how they would roll the stone away?

4. Read Ephesians 2:8-10. How do grace, faith, and good works mesh together in the Christian life?

5. What should be the balance between waiting on the Lord to bring you a spouse and acting in faith as you search for a spouse? What are your thoughts about this?

Chapter 4
Does Your Sin and Satan's Temptation Cancel Out God's Sovereign Plan for Your Future Marriage?

"God loves you!" You've heard it before, especially if you were exposed to the kind of Christian teaching I received throughout my childhood.

These three words formed the overall message I learned about God as a child. It seemed that for every Sunday school lesson, every religion class at the Christian academy I attended, and every time someone told me about God, the summary statement was "God really loves you."

This is an incredible message to grow up knowing. So please don't get me wrong — if you are a millennial like me, we should be deeply grateful for the generation before us that built ministries upon this amazing biblical truth. It is wonderfully, unfathomably true, "God loves you!" But when we are hit in the face by real life, we can't stop with "God loves you." We must take the next step and ask ourselves, *"How* does God love me?"

If we don't ask this question, we inevitably interpret God's love for us through our own personal definitions of love. Then, when the details of our lives (or the details of our relationships) do not match those definitions we have for "God's love", we stumble. If your season of singleness is more painful than you want, if your dating life has been tough, or if you have not met your future spouse in the timing that you thought this would take place, it is easy to start doubting what we've been told about God's love for us.

This occurs when we don't know "how" God loves us in his sovereignty.

One common question that arises in the human mind when we start to think about our loving, all-powerful God is, "Why does he allow sin, Satan, and evil to happen in my life if he is powerful enough to stop it all? Why does he allow bad things to happen that negatively affect my relationships? Why is he taking so long to allow me to get married?"

If we have a poor understanding of how God loves us, at best we walk away confused when our lives and relationships are not what we had hoped. At worst, as so many young people are doing, we walk away from God completely, assuming he is not loving like we have been told — or perhaps not real at all.

God Always Has a Purpose for Your Pain

I was ten years old the day my world changed. "There's something I have to tell you," my mom said as the tears began to well up and her voice began to tremble. "Your dad is in the hospital. He had a massive stroke." That's all she could get out before bursting into tears.

My dad was supposed to die that day. Through the grace of God, he actually survived. But the harm had been done — he had severe brain damage, and none of our lives would ever be same. What made matters even more confusing was that when the time came for me to sort through my parents' divorce once I got older, my dad was so different than the man he was when he was married to my mom it felt impossible to talk with him about what really happened. It was all so confusing. If God loved me, why did all this happen?

For the next several years, I struggled to reconcile the truth that God loves me with the reality of my family's pain. It took over a decade for me to find the answers I was looking for, but when I really began to understand John 11:1-6, I finally began to properly interpret my pain through the lens of God's love. The answers in this passage are not easy, but when we take these verses at face value, they are extremely beautiful and healing. These verses hold the answers our hearts are looking for as we seek to embrace God's love while also being honest about the pain we each experience.

God does indeed love us, but his love often looks so different from what we expect. The reason we doubt God's sovereign plan when we experience pain is because we often believe God's love will always cause the easiest, most pleasurable things to happen in our lives. But this is not always the case:

> "Now a certain man was ill, Lazarus of Bethany, the village of Mary and her sister Martha. [2] It was Mary who anointed the Lord with ointment and wiped his feet with her hair, whose brother Lazarus was ill. [3] So the sisters sent to him, saying, 'Lord, he whom you love is ill.' [4] But when Jesus heard it he said, 'This illness does not lead to death. It is for the glory of God, so that the Son of God may be glorified through it.'

> [5] Now Jesus loved Martha and her sister and Lazarus. [6] So, when he heard that Lazarus was ill, he stayed two days longer in the place where he was."

The last two sentences are perhaps the two most shocking sentences linked together in all of Scripture. Most of us just don't know what to do with these verses, especially with the word "*so*" that starts verse 6. Jesus loved Lazarus and his family, *so* he let Lazarus die? What are you supposed to do with that?

Well, in the 1984 NIV Bible translation, which I grew up reading, they just changed "so" to "yet." It reads, "Jesus loved Martha and her sister and Lazarus. *Yet* when he heard that Lazarus was sick, he stayed where he was two more days." In the NLT, the translators added an "although": "So *although* Jesus loved Martha, Mary, and Lazarus, he stayed where he was for the next two days."

But as the updated NIV and ESV show us, a proper Greek translation calls for a simple "so" or "therefore" at the beginning of verse 6. I believe we come up with these alternative ways of translating this verse because our understanding of the way God loves us is so different from what John writes here. It's easy to just assume there is a translation issue since it seems to make no sense in our human minds that Jesus let Lazarus die because he loves him.

The problem is that we are trying to jam our understanding of God's love into this verse, and it's just not fitting. The word is clearly "so" and we must deal with that. Jesus loved this family, *so* he let them experience pain. We have to let that sink in.

Apparently, God's love is not expressed at its greatest and highest form by saving us from trials but instead by glorifying himself through our trials.

God's Highest Form of Love

God's love for you is always expressed in its highest form when Jesus Christ is glorified in your life. This is what John 11:1–6 teaches us. God loved Lazarus, so God glorified himself by exalting Jesus Christ through Lazarus. Lazarus's greatest need was not to be healed, but to see the glory of the Son of God. Likewise, marriage is good, meeting the one is good, but when Jesus is glorified in our lives we are experiencing God's best for us.

And because God loves you and me just as much as he loves Lazarus, God's plan for us is the same. The details will be unique for each of us, but God's definition of love doesn't change. God is always willing to allow short-term pain to produce eternal glory and pleasure through Jesus Christ in those he loves.

God has not promised you a perfect life on this earth. You might never get married. Your marriage might not be the healthiest. Your spouse could die just a few years after you get married. Does this mean God is cruel because he is sovereign and could have stopped all this?

If you learn to see God's love for you through the lens of God's glory in your life — in both trials and triumph, in both boredom and excitement, in both pain and pleasure, in both singleness and marriage — you will experience the freedom Jesus came to give. When your joy is no longer tied to your relationship status but to the life of Christ, you will be free to live with happiness no matter what is going on in your life.

You may not have everything you want on this earth, but you can have all of Christ.

God Uses Satan for Your Sanctification

With just a quick read of Scripture, there's no doubt that God not only allows Satan to live, but God allows Satan to tempt us. But why does God allow Satan to tempt us when God has the power to stop the devil?

It's a good place to start by noting that any question that starts with "Why does God . . . ?" can always be answered "For his own glory and our good." Everything God does ultimately is rooted in his sovereign plan of glorifying himself and loving people.

It's also important to note that Satan is at the mercy of God's control. God uses Satan, Satan works for God, and Satan can only do what God allows him to do. Therefore, if we hold to the premises that everything God does (and allows) is for his glory and our good, and God allows Satan to tempt Christians, we can also state that God uses demonic attacks for God's glory and the Christian's good.

There are countless ways God uses the works of Satan for his will of glorifying himself and doing what's best for us. One specific way can be seen through the timing of Satan's temptations. Have you ever noticed that Satan seems to consistently tempt us during two very specific points in our life: 1. When we are tired and beaten up. 2. When we are seeking to do something meaningful for God. Notice when Jesus was tempted by the devil:

> "And Jesus, full of the Holy Spirit, returned from the Jordan and was led by the Spirit in the wilderness [2] for forty days, being tempted by the devil. And he ate nothing during those days. And when they were ended, he was hungry. [3] The devil said to him, 'If you are the Son of God, command this stone to become bread.'" (Luke 4:1-3)

Here Jesus is clearly in a physically depleted moment. The Bible noticeably states that Jesus "was hungry." Notice too that this forty days of temptation in the wilderness took place just before Jesus' public ministry began (Luke 4:14-15). In most Bible translations the headings in Luke 4 state "The Temptation of Jesus" (Luke 4:1-13) and then "Jesus Begins His Ministry" (Luke 4:14-15). Here we can see that God allowed Satan to tempt Jesus at the two specific points we all are consistently tempted during: when we are tired and when we are seeking to do something important for God.

Why on earth would God allow Satan to tempt those he loves during these two pivotal points? Satan desires to tempt at these points because he knows at these points we need God most. God allows Satan to tempt at these moments for the same reason, because he knows now more than ever we need him most. According to Scripture, how are we to resist the devil? By seeking and submitting to God: "Submit yourselves therefore to God. Resist the devil, and he will flee from you" (James 4:7).

God allows Satan to tempt us so we will seek more of God. God uses Satan to accomplish his will, and God's will is always to bring himself more glory through his people loving, pursuing, and seeking him more. Satan is used by God for this very purpose. When you are tired, you need God more than ever. When you are about to do something significant for the Kingdom of God, you need God more than ever. Is it any wonder then why God allows Satan to tempt us during these vulnerable moments? God uses Satan like God used the thorn in Paul's flesh:

> "So to keep me from becoming conceited because of the surpassing greatness of the revelations, a thorn was given me in the flesh, a messenger of Satan to harass me, to keep me from becoming conceited. [8] Three times I pleaded with the Lord about this, that it should leave me. [9] But he said to me, 'My grace is sufficient for you, for my power is made perfect in weakness.' Therefore I will boast all the more gladly of my weaknesses, so that the power of Christ may rest upon me. [10] For the sake of Christ, then, I am content with weaknesses, insults, hardships, persecutions, and calamities. For when I am weak, then I am strong." (2 Corinthians 12:7-10)

God used Satan "to keep [Paul] from becoming conceited," to cause Paul to seek God in prayer ("three times I pleaded with the Lord"), and to give Paul more power through relying on Christ in a deeper way ("For when I am weak, then I am strong").

This is God's purpose for Satan and temptation in our lives too. When you want to live a holy life, when you want a healthy Christian relationship, and when you want to glorify God in your future marriage, God must prepare and sanctify you. Sanctification is the *process* of being made holy. When we become Christians we don't just know how to live perfectly. We are given the perfection of Christ and are completely justified. However, we must learn to be sanctified and God trains us in these ways through trials and temptations.

Jesus was hungry and tired in Luke 4. Jesus was about to embark on the most important mission in the history of the universe. It was then that God used Satan for his own purpose. God used Satan in Jesus' earthly life to help Jesus love and glorify the Father more. Hebrews 5:8 affirms that even Jesus learned through suffering, "Although [Jesus] was a son, he learned obedience through what he suffered." And God uses Satan in our lives for the same reason.

Though Satan acts on his own volition, for Satan to do anything, God must allow it. God is in complete and sovereign control over the devil. God said in Jeremiah 29:13, "You will seek me and find me, when you seek me with all your heart." God helps us seek him with all our heart by any means necessary, including through the temptations of Satan.

God Is Sovereign Over Your Sin

Perhaps one of the most profound theological topics we can discuss is the relationship between God's sovereignty and man's sin. How can a sovereign God be truly in control of everything when sin happens and yet the Bible says man, not God, is fully responsible for sin?

We touched on this topic already in Chapter 2, so I won't go too into this right now. But what is important to note in this chapter is that although God never causes your sin he is still in control even when you do sin. When we are discussing this topic of man's sin and God's sovereignty, I believe "control" is a more important word than "cause." God doesn't have to be the cause of sin for God to be in control of sin. God never causes someone to act sinful, but God is still in control of all sinners, "The LORD works out everything to its proper end-- even the wicked for a day of disaster" (Proverbs 16:4, NIV).

When it comes to sin, God's sovereignty, and Christian relationships, the most relevant question I see many people ask is, "Why didn't God stop me from sinning if he knew how badly this sin would hurt me and other people? Why won't God stop me from messing up if he knows this sin will hurt my marriage one day?"

Perhaps you had premarital sex, perhaps you did something wrong and you lost a relationship that you really cared about, or perhaps someone's sin against you has negatively impacted your ability to have the type of relationship you want. Why didn't God stop sin in your life so you could have fewer problems in relationships, less problems meeting the one, or less problems that might occur in your future because of the sins of you past? If God is sovereign, why didn't he stop us from our sins?

There are many answers we could give. The most important answer, however, is that God didn't use his sovereign power to stop your sin because he used his sovereign power to send us our Savior instead. The goals you feel that are ruined because of your sin can still be accomplished through the gospel.

God doesn't show his power by never allowing us to die. God will ultimately show his power by raising us from the dead. Likewise, God doesn't need to stop you from sinning in order to accomplish his sovereign will. God will accomplish his sovereign will for your life and your relationships not through your perfection but through the perfections of Christ, through the gospel. He is powerful enough to redeem you rather than stop your sin.

God shows his glory and power in a greater way by accomplishing his plan without micromanaging your behavior. It is a greater expression of power and glory for God to bring about his will even when he allows people to exercise their wills. We could all understand how God could accomplish his will if he was pulling the strings like a puppet master and everything you were doing was actually not your choice. But how do you fully grasp the power of the God who brings about his good will for you even though he allows us to sin? Now that is power!

The glory of the gospel is not that God stops us from sin but that he saves us from our sins. If you think your life is over and you can never have a successful relationship because of your sin, you are selling your Savior short. If you think you blew God's plan for your life because of your sin, you are saying your sin is greater than God's grace. You may need to adjust your perspective of what your life will look like. But God's sovereign plan is greater than your sin because his grace is greater than anything you can ever do.

God didn't have to stop you from your sin. He sent Jesus instead. Jesus came through a perfect birth, he lived a perfect life, he died a perfect death, he was raised in perfection, and when we put our faith in Jesus and repent of sin, through God's grace we get the perfections of Jesus placed on us. Jesus saving you through the gospel is God's sovereign plan for you (Ephesians 1:3-14).

So neither Satan nor your sin can separate you from the love of God (Romans 8:37-39). Because of your sinful past you may not be able to fathom how God will bring about your marriage or sustain you in your singleness, but I imagine Mary and Martha didn't know how Jesus was going to fix everything either once their brother died. They had to let Jesus work his resurrection power. If they had walked away half way through the story and abandoned Jesus they would never have seen Lazarus rise from the dead.

You must give God time to work his sovereign plan. You must allow him time to sanctify you through the trials and temptations of life. I don't know his specific plan for your marriage or for your life of singleness. But I do know your sin does not rule out God's sovereign plan. If you don't rely on the gospel, you have no hope. But if you do rely on the gospel, never underestimate the power of his grace to bring good out of what was meant for evil.

(Note: Some of the information in this chapter was taken from an article I wrote for DesiringGod.org called, *Where Is God's Love in Loss?* Also, if you want more information on the topics covered in this chapter, you might really enjoy my other book, *Intertwined: Our Happiness Is Tied to God's Glory.*)

Reflection Questions:

1. Why is it important to not only know that God loves us but to also know "how" God loves us?

2. Read John 11:1-6. What is significant about this passage to you?

3. If Satan's temptations and our sin can damage our relationships and future marriage, why does God allow these things to happen?

4. What is God's solution to sin? Explain. What Bible verses help you answer this question?

5. If someone asked you, "Does my sin and Satan's temptation cancel out God's plan for my future marriage?" how would you answer?

Chapter 5
Why Pray About Your Future Marriage in Your Singleness If God Is Sovereign?

As we have been discussing, when we begin to learn about God's sovereignty, the temptation is to turn into the "frozen chosen" who use God's power as an excuse to be lazy. If God is in total control of everything, why pray at all? What benefit is there to pray about your future marriage as a single person if God already has a preordained plan for how you will meet, date, and marry the one he has for you?

Certainly prayer and God's power is a multi-layered topic that could be talked about endlessly in the theological classroom. But a more practical concern arises when a belief in God's sovereignty causes you to pray less. This is not what God wants.

So to answer the question, "Why pray if God is sovereign?", perhaps a counter question will help us see the Bible's answer: Why would you pray if God was not sovereign?

God's Sovereign Plan Is Why Praying in Your Singleness About Your Marriage Makes Sense

God's sovereignty is not a reason to pray less, work less, evangelize less – God's sovereignty should motivate us to do all of these things more. Because he is all powerful we can step out in faith. If God wasn't all powerful, putting our faith in him would make no sense.

People ask "Why pray if God is sovereign?" because the common response to learning about God's sovereignty is to feel like a mindless robot with no freedom. A God with complete control seems oppressive. But God wants us to feel the opposite. Nowhere does the Bible says that because God is sovereign man is not free. Again, the opposite is true. Because God is sovereign, man can be free.

When God saves us through the gospel, he doesn't violate our freewill. He sets our will free. We are slaves to sin until Jesus sets us free (Romans 6:20-23). When Jesus sets us free, then we freely choose to follow a new Master. Galatians 5:1 explains, "For freedom Christ has set us free; stand firm therefore, and do not submit again to a yoke of slavery." Because Christ has set us free, now we must willingly choose to live free, actively choosing not to allow ourselves to live under a yoke of slavery. Just because Christ has set you free doesn't mean you are living free. According to Galatians 5:1, that's your *choice* to make.

The biblical truth of God's sovereignty should not deflate your prayer life and cause you to pray less about the hopes you have for a relationship. God's supreme power should cause you to pray more. Again, if God was powerless to do whatever he wanted, why pray at all? Prayer to God would be foolish if man was in total control.

Praying is a confession that you do believe in the sovereignty of God. When you pray about meeting the one and when you pray about your future marriage, you are confessing that you believe in God's power to bring it all into existence. So if you find yourself struggling to pray, perhaps it is because you have overemphasized the power of man and underemphasized the sovereignty of God to move on your behalf.

Prayer Is a Confession of Your Belief in God's Sovereignty

In J.I. Packer's book, *Evangelism and the Sovereignty of God*, he addresses the logical roadblocks that occur when we embrace God's election and then struggle to see the point of evangelizing. The common thought is "If the only way to be saved is to be chosen, then who cares if we tell people about Jesus anyway?"

Throughout Packer's book, he makes the point that God's sovereignty is not a reason to evangelize less. It is the reason to evangelize more. I'll let you read his book on your own to hear his full arguments, but how he begins this book relates perfectly to the questions, "Why pray if God is sovereign?" The opening lines of his first chapter state:

> "I do not intend to spend any time at all proving to you the general truth that God is sovereign in His world. There is no need; for I know that, if you are a Christian, you believe this already. How do I know that? Because I know that, if you are a Christian, you pray; and the recognition of God's sovereignty is the basis of your prayers. In prayer, you ask for things and give thanks for things. Why? Because you recognize that God is the author and source of all the good that you have had already, and all the good that you hope for in the future. This is the fundamental philosophy of Christian prayer. . . In effect, therefore, what we do every time we pray is to confess our own impotence and God's sovereignty. The very fact that a Christian prays is thus proof positive that he believes in the Lordship of his God."

Let's take Packer's point a step further. If prayer "is to confess our own impotence and God's sovereignty," is it not safe to also say that a lack of prayer is to confess our unbelief of God's sovereignty and a belief in our own power? Our beliefs about God will manifest in our prayer life.

In Matthew 6:9 when Jesus teaches us the Lord's Prayer, the first line in the prayer is "Our Father in heaven." Jesus is seeking to remind us that we should pray because our Father is reigning over the earth, able to bring about whatever he wills as he sits on his throne in heaven. "Our Father" is an intimate term, motivating us to pray because of God's fatherly love for us. But the next phrase, "who art in heaven," shows God's supremacy, motivating us to pray because of God's authority as the Preeminent King over all of his creation. Both facts, God's love and sovereignty, should motivate us to pray.

In the Lord's Prayer, Jesus then says "Your kingdom come, your will be done." Jesus' prayer would make no sense if God could not actually bring about his will and his kingdom whenever he wanted to do it.

So rather than allowing the sovereignty of God to cause you to pray less about meeting the one and less about having a healthy future marriage, the Bible says that the sovereignty of God is the reason you *should* pray about these types of things.

God Uses Prayer to Change Your Circumstances

The first way prayer changes things is by God answering your prayers and changing the circumstances in your life.

For example, Jesus prayed, "Abba, Father, everything is possible for you. Take this cup from me. Yet not what I will, but what you will" (Mark 14:36). The first part of Jesus' request is what most of us think about when we think of how prayer helps us. Jesus said, "Take this cup from me." Prayer helps because sometimes God does change the world around us. Everything is possible for God. Sometimes he does spare us of painful trials, sometimes he does heal our sicknesses, and sometimes he does give us a more enjoyable work environment. And yes, sometimes God does just answer your prayer for a godly spouse and brings that person into your life.

It is right to ask God for the things you want. All over Scripture we are instructed to ask God. Right in Mark 14:36 Jesus himself is asking his Father for what he wanted. In one respect, Jesus clearly did not want to bear the shame of the cross. In Hebrews 12:2 we are told that Jesus scorned the shame of the cross. He was not skipping along on the road to Golgotha with a smile as if it was no skin off his back. The thought of bearing the sins of the world was anguish for Jesus. The text says in Luke 22:44 that Jesus' pain before the cross was so severe that his sweat became like drops of blood. Jesus says in Mark 14:34 that his soul was overwhelmed with sorrow almost to the point of death.

So of course it was right for Jesus to ask that if it were possible, that this cup of suffering might pass. Likewise, it is right for us to pray that God might change the troubles and temptations in the world around us. It is right to ask God for the ways you wish your life circumstances would change. If you want to be married, you should pray that God would allow you to be married. If you want a healthy marriage one day, then you should be praying about this right now.

You Should Pray About Meeting and Marrying Your Future Spouse Because God Uses Prayer to Change You and Prepare You for His Sovereign Plan

The second part of Jesus' prayer in Mark 14:36, however, is an element of prayer that most of us probably think far less about but perhaps is given more emphasis in the Bible. Jesus said, "Yet not what I will, but what you will." Prayer can be used by God to change the world around us, but more often than not God uses prayer to change what is happening inside of us.

God uses prayer more often not to change our world every time we ask him, but rather to conform the person praying to the plan that he already has for him or her. First Jesus prayed that the external circumstances would change for him, which is right and biblical to do. But then he also submits himself to the preordained will of God. He not only prays about the temptation, in prayer he prepares himself to handle the temptation correctly. Perhaps God is not in heaven constantly changing what he has planned when we pray about it, but perhaps he desires us to pray so he can prepare our hearts for the plans he already has for us.

Romans 8:28 is perhaps one of the most famous verses in the Bible. If you go into the Christian bookstores, 50% of the their beautiful and very classy trinkets will have this verse on them, "And we know that in all things God works for the good of those who love him, who have been called according to his purpose." It's a beautiful verse. It's an amazing promise that should bring us comfort. When bad things happen, God can work them out for our good. But to really appreciate what God is saying we must keep reading, for Romans 8:29 states, "For those God foreknew he also predestined to be conformed to the image of his Son, that he might be the firstborn among many brothers and sisters."

God works everything out for our good not ultimately because God will do everything that we pray, but rather through our prayers God is going to change us. When we come into the presence of God, we are not there so we can change the mind of God but rather that our minds might be changed by him. God conforms us to the image of his Son. We are not conforming God. God is the potter and we are the clay, and one of God's primary tools for molding us is prayer.

Romans 12:2 states, "Do not conform to the pattern of this world, but be transformed by the renewing of your mind. Then you will be able to test and approve what God's will is—his good, pleasing and perfect will." Again, God conforms us to his perfect will.

For example, when you pray for your future spouse now before you even know him or her, it prepares your heart to love your future spouse in your future marriage. Praying for someone not only benefits that person because through those prayers God is filling your heart with more love for that person you are praying for.

Intercessory prayer benefits you as the intercessor too because praying for another causes you to exercise your heart muscles for that person. Like physical muscles, the more we use our spiritual muscles the stronger they get. When you use your spiritual love muscles in prayer for your future spouse, you are strengthening your love for your future spouse before you even meet him or her. Praying for the health of your future marriage prepares you for that marriage and makes you healthier, which will then cause your marriage to be healthier once it comes into existence one day. Compassion and love for others is a trait that can grow in us when we cultivate it and work at it. So when you pray for your future spouse you are cultivating a heart within yourself that will be ready to serve your spouse in your future marriage.

So you should pray about meeting and marrying the one God has for you because through your prayers God will mold you into the person he wants you to be before he can bless you. He will not bless us with gifts that we are not ready to handle with care and wisdom. He will not give you the heart of his daughter or the heart of his son if you have not prepared yourself to love his child well. When you pray about your future marriage, you are giving God the opportunity to prepare you for your future marriage.

God Does Not Spare Us of Every Unwanted Season, but He Does Promise to Be with Us in Every Season

The Father heard the cries of Jesus, and he answered Jesus. But that doesn't mean he was spared the cup of suffering as was asked by Jesus. God did not spare Jesus the death on the cross, but he saved him out of death through the resurrection. Likewise, God does not spare us of suffering and temptation, but he does have the power to save us out of anything we endure.

Nowhere in the Scriptures does God promise us that our lives and relationships will be just the way we want. He doesn't promise that all our prayers for a future marriage will happen just as we prayed them and as soon as we pray them. But God does promise us that he is able to sustain us through the pain, temptation, unwanted singleness, and the loneliness we might feel. God has not promised to stop the storms. He hasn't promised to change all our outer problems around us. But he has promised that he will bring us safely through the storm if we rely on him.

Jesus never told Peter that he could avoid temptation, "Watch and pray that you may not enter into temptation" (Mark 14:38). He told Peter to pray so that he would not fall into temptation. God does not spare us of the trials and temptations we encounter on earth, but he does desire to deliver us out of them (1 Corinthians 10:13). These truths apply to difficult seasons of life too. Singleness is harder to deal with for some. But God can comfort you through it if you rely on him.

Because we know God controls our future, we can trust him in our present.

(Note: If you enjoyed this chapter and would like to learn more about the link between God's sovereign power and prayer, you may enjoy my other book, *Never Quit: 5 Powerful Prayer Truths from Luke 18:1-8 that Can Completely Transform Your Prayer Life.*)

Reflection Questions:

1. If God is sovereign and has a plan for how you will meet, date, and marry your future spouse, what's the point of praying about all this?

2. What are the two ways that prayer changes our lives?

3. How does praying about your future marriage and for your future spouse in your singleness benefit the health of that relationship before it even comes into existence?

4. Read Mark 14:36, Romans 8:28-29, and Romans 12:2. What pattern do you see in these Bible verses?

5. In your own words, do you feel it is important to pray about your future marriage? Why or why not?

Chapter 6
Why Is God Waiting to Show You the Date He Has Set for Your Wedding Day?

God alone has the power to give you a godly marriage, and prayer is our primary way of making specific requests of our Heavenly Father. So as we discussed in the previous chapter, you should pray about meeting, dating, and marrying the person God has planned for you to marry.

But why does God not answer some of these prayers about relationships the way we want and when we want? God loves us, he hears us, and prayer really works. But sometimes our prayers go "unanswered"? Why? Did we do something wrong? Did we not pray the correct way? Did we not pray enough? Is God just fickle and unexplainable sometimes?

There are many answers to questions like these, but by studying Mark 10:35-40, we can see at least three answers to why God does not answer some prayers.

(As a point of clarification, in this chapter I'm operating under the principle that God hears and answers every prayer with either a yes, no, or not yet. So throughout this chapter when I use the language of "Why does God not answer some prayers?", what I mean is "Why does God not answer some prayers the way we want and when we want?" We know he answers every prayer one way or the other, but why does God not give us what we ask for sometimes?)

1. God Does Not Answer Some Prayers Because He Cares Too Much

> "And James and John, the sons of Zebedee, came up to him and said to him, 'Teacher, we want you to do for us whatever we ask of you.' [36]And he said to them, 'What do you want me to do for you?'" (Mark 10:35-36).

I can identify with how James and John started their request, "God, before I ask the specifics, I want to get you to agree that you will say "yes" to whatever I say next." While this seems like something a young child would try to pull with their parents, so often this is our mentality when we pray about relationships. We may not articulate it that way, but when we get upset at God when he does not do what we want, we show we have a subconscious belief that if God really cared, he would do whatever we asked.

The reason God does not answer some prayers is simply because God loves us too much to give us a blank check. If a parent did just say, "Yeah, yeah . . . do whatever you want," and said "yes" to any request the child had, this would not be an act of love but of neglect. My children have asked me for some outrageous things, "Dad, can we get a lion? Dad, can I get a real sword? Dad, can I just eat candy for dinner?" What kind of father would I be if I granted every request my children brought to me? Likewise, God does not just give us a blank check because he cares too much about us to do that.

In love, God is always available. Like a loving parent, Jesus expresses his love not by saying "yes" to anything but by graciously listening and weighing through what we have to say, "What do you want me to do for you?" (Mark 10:36). That's what Jesus said to his disciples and that's what God says to us. He doesn't say, "I'll do whatever you want." He says, "Tell me what you want and let's talk about it. I will do what's best for you because I love you."

When you pray about your desires in relationships, this is the approach God takes with you. If God does not give you what you want, you can assume it's because he loves you too much and knows something you don't know.

2. God Does Not Answer Some Prayers Because We Are Not Omniscient Like Him

> "And they said to him, 'Grant us to sit, one at your right hand and one at your left, in your glory.' [38]Jesus said to them, 'You do not know what you are asking. Are you able to drink the cup that I drink, or to be baptized with the baptism with which I am baptized?'" (Mark 10:37-38)

I deeply appreciate Jesus' thoughtful, kind answer to this request, "You do not know what you are asking." Imagine if God answered every prayer by high school students when they ask him to allow a certain relationship to happen. Imagine how many problems we would endure in our relationships if God just did what we asked rather than doing what was best for us because he knows the full scope of what we are really requesting.

Sometimes the scariest thing is when we keep rejecting God's "no", but we keep persisting in a certain prayer, and God grants our request because we just won't move on with him until we get what we want. The results are always disastrous. God warned the Israelites how disastrous it would be if he gave them a human king like they wanted, and yet the people just wouldn't let it go. So God finally gave them what they wanted and they suffered the consequences (1 Samuel 8).

If you are committed to being with this one specific person and you refuse to listen to God, sometimes God allows you to be with him or her to show you why he kept telling you "No." Because you are stuck and have dug your heels in, he gets you unstuck by teaching you the hard way. God always prefers to teach us the easy way, but he will teach us one way or the other.

God does not answer some prayers because he knows everything and we do not. There's just so much we don't know. But what we do know is that God loves us, cares for us, and hears our prayers. Thus whatever the outcome, we can be certain that God has our best interest at heart. We do not always know what we are really asking for, but God always does. Thankfully he alone is the final decision maker on what prayers are answered.

So when God does not answer our prayers, it might be confusing, but when you really think about it, you should thank him for sparing you of the problems you don't even know that he is sparing you from. We don't always know why God says no to certain requests, but we know that God always does what is best for his glory and our good. We can find comfort and peace when we accept that sometimes God says to us, "You do not know what you ask" (Mark 10:38). God knows all, therefore we can trust him at all times.

3. God Does Not Answer Some Prayers Because He Has to Prepare Us for a Particular Future First

> "And they said to him, 'We are able.' And Jesus said to them, 'The cup that I drink you will drink, and

with the baptism with which I am baptized, you will be baptized, ^{40} but to sit at my right hand or at my left is not mine to grant, but it is for those for whom it has been prepared.'" (Mark 10:39-40)

Sometimes God does not say "yes" or "no" but rather "not yet." James and John thought they were asking to rule with Jesus in their present season in an earthly kingdom. Little did they know that if they wanted to be at Jesus' right and left hand, they would have to suffer with Jesus.

When Jesus asked James and John if they were ready to suffer with him, they answered "We are able." But Jesus essentially answered "you will" be ready eventually. Jesus knew that right now, they were not ready to do what they would be called to do later. James and John still needed training, they still needed the power of the Holy Spirit to enter into them, and they were not quite ready to do what they would later be called to do.

So God does not answer some prayers about the desires you have for a relationship because he first needs to prepare you for what lies ahead in the future. God knew what he had planned for James and John but needed to prepare them for the future he had for them. Likewise God knows what he has planned for you, but he sometimes does not give you that future right when you ask for it because he has to prepare you for it. Often God will say "yes" to our prayer only after he spends time developing us and empowering us to handle the blessing he plans to give.

God has a plan for the world and for each one of our lives. If a prayer request contradicts God's sovereign plan, God will not answer that request. The most powerful prayers are those that are in alignment with God's will (1 John 5:14-15). Even

Jesus did not always have his prayer requests answered the way he wanted, for as Matthew 26:39 explains, Jesus prayed, "My Father, if it be possible, let this cup pass from me; nevertheless, not as I will, but as you will."

Jesus qualified his request with "if it be possible." All things are possible with God. So what did Jesus mean? He meant that if this prayer request fits into God's sovereign plan, he would like it granted. But Jesus' greater desire was not to have his own way but to do the will of his Father. So God does not answer some of our prayers because God always has a sovereign plan. We are not robots mindlessly plugging along. Your prayers about a relationship really do change things. Your prayers really do matter and are positively affecting your future marriage. But we don't always know what God's plan is, so when your prayers don't fit God's foreordained will for your life, God does not override his plan with your plan.

Jesus didn't know if James and John's request could be granted, ". . . but to sit at my right or left is not for me to grant. These places belong to those for whom they have been prepared" (Mark 10:40, NIV). Sometimes we all need to just wait for God's will to be revealed. One day God's plan for your marriage will be revealed and it will all make sense. In the meantime, we can seek to echo the faithful heart of Jesus, "Not as I will, but as you will."

How to Pray About Your Hope for a Future Marriage

As I mentioned in the introduction, this book is not meant to be a step-by-step guide on how to meet, date, and get married. I believe in practical application and have been holding back throughout this book because once I get started it's hard for me to stop. This book would be triple its size if we started down that road. My main goal in this book is to help you trust and know God's plan for you. So far we have been talking about the trusting part. In the next chapter we will be transitioning into the "knowing part" and we will be answering "How will you know when you meet the one God has for you?"

So at this point it seems like a natural fit to include some practical ways to pray if you hope to be married. You will want to read some of my other books, visit ApplyGodsWord.com, or visit my YouTube channel if you really want some practical tips for Christian singleness and dating. Below, however, are five specific ways you can pray for a Christian spouse.

1. If You Want a Christian Marriage, Just Pray, "Lord, I ask that you would bring a godly spouse into my life."

This first point is really important.

Prayer isn't about punching in the right combination of words that will unlock God's blessings. So when you have a desire, you should ask God for it in the most direct way possible. Quiet your heart, focus on God, and just ask him for what you want, "Lord, I ask that you would bring a godly spouse into my life." 1 John 5:14-15 states:

> "And this is the confidence that we have toward him, that if we ask anything according to his will he hears us. [15] And if we know that he hears us in whatever we ask, we know that we have the requests that we have asked of him."

Marriage is a good thing that is biblical, therefore it is right to pray about being married if this is a desire on your heart.

There's no guarantee that God will answer your prayer the way you want or in the timing that you want. Notice it says that God will only answer our prayers when they are "according to his will." Even though God may not answer your prayer for a spouse with a "yes" (although he may), he still commands us to pray about everything. Philippians 4:6-7 states:

> "Do not be anxious about anything, but in every situation, by prayer and petition, with thanksgiving, present your requests to God. ⁷ And the peace of God, which transcends all understanding, will guard your hearts and your minds in Christ Jesus."

When you pray that God would give you a godly spouse, he may or may not give you one. But anytime you pray, God will take away your anxiety and replace it with the peace of Christ.

2. To Receive a Godly Spouse, Pray That God Would Reveal the Flaws in You

If you want a godly spouse, this point is so crucial.

One reason God often withholds his blessings is because we are not ready to receive those blessings because of our personal sin. Perhaps God does want to bless you with a godly spouse, but he can't answer this prayer because there is sin in your life that will sabotage your marriage.

I'm not saying you earn blessings because of your good behavior or don't earn blessing because of your bad behavior. I'm just saying that God loves us too much to bless us with gifts we can't handle. If there is a character flaw in you that will cause you to ruin the godly relationship you are praying for, in kindness God may be delaying this relationship until you mature enough to handle it.

The faster you mature, the faster God will be able to bless you with what he already plans to give you. Therefore, if you want a godly spouse, pray that God would reveal any flaws in you that may be blocking his blessing. Spend time in confession every day and reflect on the areas of your life where you know you need improvement. Pray Psalm 139:23-24, "Search me, O God, and know my heart! Try me and know my thoughts! And see if there is any grievous way in me, and lead me in the way everlasting!"

3. Pray that God Would Prepare Your Spouse's Heart for Marriage Too

Without this only half the puzzle is complete.

While you may need to grow to have a successful marriage, the same may be true of your future spouse as well. Therefore you should pray for his or her heart as well.

Pray that God would help your future spouse, whoever he or she may be, to live for God. Pray that they would be quick to repent of their sin, that they would stay clear of damaging relationships, that they would seek to obey God, and that they would take the time they need to develop into the person God wants them to be.

If you want a godly spouse, start praying for that specific person God has for you even though you don't even know his or her name yet.

4. If You Want a Godly Spouse, Pray that God Would Give You Discernment to See Good Potential Godly Spouses

One quality that will speed up or slow down your future marriage from happening is your ability to discern the character and maturity of other people.

If you waste your time dating a lot of people who are not good candidates to be a godly spouse, you are delaying your marriage. To increase the speed of your Christian marriage forming, you should only date the type of people who will actually be godly spouses one day. Why date people who don't even seem to have the potential right now to be a godly spouse at all, let alone your godly spouse?

To do this wisely, you will need discernment. Discernment is the ability to see things not for how they appear but for how they truly are. Discerning people are those who can sense red flags before others, who can pick up on unhealthy behavior, and who are able to see the differences in those who are mature or immature.

Discernment can look a lot like judgment, but these two things are very different. The main difference occurs in how they are used. When you sinfully judge someone, you assume things about them that are not true or you look down on them because you know something negative about them. Discernment is about gauging the evidence you have and making the best decision possible without looking down on others.

If you want to marry a godly spouse, pray for the discernment to know who are good candidates to get to know and who are people you shouldn't consider dating.

5. Pray God's Word If You Want a Godly Spouse

This last point is the most important.

As we discussed earlier, if you want your prayers answered, you must pray in alignment with God's will. God has revealed his will in his word. Therefore if you want a godly spouse, you should pray the Scriptures.

For example, if you are praying for a wife, you could pray the words in Proverbs 31:10-31. Or if you if you are praying for a husband, you could read through 1 Timothy 3:3-13 and ask God to give you a godly man as described in that Bible passage. You could read through Ephesians 5:22-33 and ask that God would make you and your future spouse into the type of people ready to fulfill the biblical roles of a husband and a wife. You could pray through Galatians 5:22-26 and ask God to help you and your future spouse be the types of people who produce the fruits of the Spirit.

You and your spouse will not match these Bible verses perfectly, but when you pray the word of God there is power in your prayers.

The Holy Spirit Is Interceding for You

Lastly, take comfort that God is all powerful. Even if you don't pray perfectly, which none of us will, the Holy Spirit is praying on our behalf the things we don't even know we should pray. Romans 8:26-27 states:

> "In the same way, the Spirit helps us in our weakness. We do not know what we ought to pray for, but the Spirit himself intercedes for us through wordless groans. [27] And he who searches our

hearts knows the mind of the Spirit, because the Spirit intercedes for God's people in accordance with the will of God."

So if you want to pray for a godly spouse, but you are not quite sure what to pray, trust that the Holy Spirit is praying for you too.

Reflection Questions:

1. What are some reasons God does not answer every prayer the exact way we ask?

2. How does God express his love through a "No" when we ask for a certain relationship to happen but it does not happen?

3. Read Mark 10:35-40. What is one takeaway you got from this passage that helps you understand praying about relationships?

4. Of the five practical ways to pray about your future marriage mentioned at the end of this chapter, which one do you feel you need to focus on the most right now?

5. Choose one Bible passage that you can pray over for your future marriage.

Chapter 7
How Will God Reveal The One to You? (Part 1: Through His Word)

There's been so many times in life where I said, "How can I hear God's voice? I just want to know what God is saying to me so I can make the right decision! Which way am I supposed to go, Lord?" When there's a big decision to make in life, you want nothing more than to simply know for certain what God is actually saying to you.

I especially remember feeling the weight and confusion of trying to hear God clearly in my young adult years because there were so many big decisions to be made at that time in life: Should I go on this mission's trip or not? Should I go to college for this degree or that one? Should I change majors or stick with the one I have? What career should I choose? Should I date her? What is a good length of time to date before being engaged? Should we get married? Should we go on this vacation or stay home? Should we buy this house or keep renting? Should we become members of this church or that one? Is it time to start having kids?

In most cases, I remember thinking, "I really don't care which option I'm supposed to choose right now. I just want to make sure I'm choosing the right one. If I could just clearly hear what God wants me to do and know for sure that's his will for me, then I could be at peace."

What I have learned over the years is that knowing God's will for your life and hearing God's voice will always have elements of faith, so we will rarely get words painted in the sky leading us with unmistakable clarity. Peace comes through trusting God no matter what, even when you are uncertain of what's ahead.

However, as Dallas Willard put it in his classic book, *Hearing God*, "Faith is not opposed to knowledge; it is opposed to sight." Therefore, while we may not always be able to "see" everything that God has planned for us (thus the need for faith, Hebrews 11:1), there are still ways to "know" which way he is leading you.

In fact, I believe there are at least three specific ways in which God speaks. God speaks through his word, through the Holy Spirit's impressions on your heart, and through the circumstances in your life. These three means of hearing God and knowing his will are the focus of these next three chapters.

God Speaks Through His Word

If you want to know what the will of God is, it starts with knowing what the word of God says.

Reading the Bible seems so conservative and modest that it almost feels like a cop-out for me to offer it as advice on how to hear God's voice about your relationships. When people talk about hearing God's voice, knowing God's will, and choosing the "right path" that God wants them to take, they are typically looking for something a bit sexier and audible compared to reading the Bible.

But studying the Bible must always be the first piece of advice when it comes to hearing God's voice and knowing his will because the Bible gives us the guardrails as we travel forward on the road of life. Doctrines may seem dogmatic, but they are foundational for our personal interactions and conversations with God. God will never tell you something that contradicts the Bible.

Perhaps so many people find the Bible boring because they don't really believe God speaks through it personally to them and their unique questions and circumstances. The Bible is exciting to read when you realize God uses it to send you personal messages of truth that directly apply to your life. Yes, the Bible is full of absolute truth, so I'm not saying each of us gets a unique truth from God. Rather, when we are listening closely to the Holy Spirit's leading, we will get personal application points, applying God's absolute truth to our very unique lives, questions, and relationships.

If Hearing God's Voice Is Not Guided By the Bible, You Will Always Doubt What You Hear

One of the problems I've noticed when it comes to hearing God's voice is not knowing whether or not we are making his voice up in our heads. How can you trust you are actually hearing God? Perhaps you just want that relationship so bad you are creating a false voice in your head and just doing what you want rather than what God is actually telling you to do.

The first way we can decipher God's personal leading in our lives is to test it against his general truths outlined in Scripture. If you ever "hear God" saying he hates you, or that he wants you to commit an act specifically forbidden in

Scripture, or that he is revealing a "new truth" that contradicts what is clearly outlined in the Bible – you are definitely not hearing God. What God says to you personally will never contradict what he has said to everyone through his written, infallible word. For example:

- If you are wondering if God is leading you to date or marry a certain person but that person is not a Christian and you are, you can be confident God is not leading you down that road because to be unequally yoked is expressly forbidden in the Bible (2 Corinthians 6:14, 1 Corinthians 7:39).
- If you get married one day but then your spouse turns out to be a false convert but still wants to remain married to you, God will not tell you to divorce him or her because the Bible says to stay married to an unbeliever if he or she wants to stay married (1 Corinthians 7:13).
- If you think God is telling you to marry someone you are not attracted to and that you really don't want to be married to, God is not saying this because the Bible says marriage is only for those who want to be married. It is not a command for all people (1 Corinthians 7:36-38).

My point is that God will never tell you to do something that contradicts his word. When it comes to hearing God's voice, however, studying the Bible is not enough. We need to read the Scriptures first with the intent of discovering the original message and meaning of the author. But the Bible is living and active (Hebrews 4;12), which means that although it is filled with unchanging, absolute truth, the Holy Spirit uses

Scripture to instruct us on personal decisions and issues unique to our individual circumstances.

How to Hear God's Voice Through the Bible

You usually won't hear God's voice through reading the Bible and finding literal words and sentences that directly inform you on your question, "Yes! Now I know I should marry my boyfriend Joe because I randomly flipped to Matthew 1:18 and it talks about Mary being betrothed to Joseph. Clearly God must be sending me that message!"

More often the Holy Spirit will teach you a truth or principle in the Bible and then help you apply that truth to your individual circumstance and relationship question. When you hear and then apply God's word you can be sure you are hearing his voice and obeying his leading.

What I am not saying is that hearing God's voice through the Bible is done the same way as shaking a magic eight ball. While playing "Bible roulette" (which is when you randomly flip the Bible open and interpret the first thing you read as God's voice to you) would be easier in some people's opinion, it would not be beneficial.

God ultimately has given us his word not as a book of rules and instructions we need to learn; rather, it is ultimately a book about a person we need to know. You could certainly do worse things than living your life strictly by biblical principles without God's intimate leading. But what is available to us through Jesus Christ is far greater than that. Because of what Jesus has done, we can boldly come into the presence of God, casting all our anxieties on him and receiving personal direction and peace in return (1 Peter 5:7). Hebrews 4:15 states, "Let us then with confidence draw near to the throne of grace, that we may receive mercy and find grace to help in time of need."

So when it comes to hearing God's voice through reading the Bible, I'm not saying you replace the intimate leading of the Holy Spirit with the physical pages of Scripture. It's not Father, Son, and Holy Bible. The Holy Spirit certainly speaks to our hearts personally. But whenever the Holy Spirit speaks, his words will always align with the Bible. The Holy Spirit wrote the Bible (through the hands and personalities of men), so it makes logical sense that what he spoke then will be consistent with what he is speaking to us now in our personal lives since God is never changing.

The Holy Spirit Speaks Through the Bible

So does the Bible or the Holy Spirit teach us everything we need to know about God? Does the Bible or the Holy Spirit lead us to an intimate relationship with the Father? Does the Bible or the Holy Spirit fill us with the power to obey and have the knowledge to please God? According to the Bible, the answer is "the Holy Spirit" to all of these questions.

What the Bible does claim, however, is that the Holy Spirit will speak through the Scriptures to teach us about God. God the Holy Spirit uses the Scriptures to guide, fill, and accomplish the Father's will in the believer's life. Without the Spirit, the Bible will not be of any service to us.

Notice that the Bible is our one weapon against Satan, but God refers to this weapon as "the sword of the Spirit, which is the word of God" (Ephesians 6:17). If we replace the Spirit's presence with the Bible, we no longer have the sword of the Spirit, we have a human sword, as we will seek to use the word of God through the wisdom of man, which will not be enough to understand and apply the real truth the Bible contains. Satan himself knows the word of God better than we ever will, and he seeks to use it for his own evil agenda. Without the Holy Spirit making us holy, we can study the Scriptures but in our sinfulness we will use our knowledge for evil and not good, just like Satan.

Since the Holy Spirit is the one who used man to write the Scriptures, the Holy Spirit is therefore the true author of the Bible (2 Peter 1:21). Therefore to be in communion with the Spirit and to know what the Spirit is speaking, we must be students of the Spirit's Scriptures. The Scriptures must always guide our personal experiences with God because we are imperfect and God's word is perfect.

God will always use his word in personally leading us. Therefore seeking the Spirit's counsel is not about God giving us extra-biblical information but rather allowing the Spirit to apply biblical wisdom in a personal way to your life.

The Holy Spirit is greater than God's Holy Scriptures. Again, this statement does not diminish the Scriptures but rather reminds us of the deity and Sovereignty of God the Holy Spirit. The Bible is living and active because the Holy Spirit wrote it through men. Without the Spirit the Scriptures would not exist. Without the Spirit no one can understand the Scriptures (2 Corinthians 2). Without the Holy Spirit we do not have the power to apply the Scriptures to our lives (Philippians 2:13).

Obeying God's word confirms that you are being led by the Spirit, "Whoever keeps his commandments abides in God, and God in him. And by this we know that he abides in us, by the Spirit whom he has given us" (1 John 3:24). While the Scriptures are the primary tool the Holy Spirit uses to speak, teach, and convict, the Holy Scriptures are still a tool God uses and not a god to be worshiped in itself.

God Will Reveal The One to You Through His Word

So now let's apply these general truths about knowing God's will through studying God's word to the question of "How will God reveal the one to me? How will I know who I am supposed to marry?"

God will not tell you who to marry specifically in his word, "Marry Amy!" But God does help us know who he wants us to marry by teaching us what *type* of person Christians should marry. To get the answers you seek about a certain person, you must ask general biblical questions about this person: Is this person a Christian? Is this person faithful? Is this person a man or woman after God's heart? Does this possible marriage union contradict any commands in Scripture?

In other words, is this potential marriage partner the type of person God tells Christians to marry in general? Will you be somewhat compatible and equally yoked theologically in marriage? Is your vision for the type of life you want to live for God compatible with one another? Answer questions like these through studying God's word and then compare your possible marriage with your findings. No one will be perfect. Each marriage will have struggles. If you are looking for perfection you will always be unmarried. But never deny obvious truths in Scripture for the sake of marrying someone.

There are many truths in Scripture that you can test a relationship against to see if it is God's will. But now I am going to give you my top three biblical qualities I believe you should look for in a person to know whether or not they might be the person God wants you to marry.

The first quality the Bible says your spouse will have if you are a Christian seeking to obey God's will is salvation. If you are a Christian, the person God wants you to marry is also a Christian. 1 Corinthians 7:39 (NIV) states, "A woman is bound to her husband as long as he lives. But if her husband dies, she is free to marry anyone she wishes, but he must belong to the Lord." You can marry who you want, as long as he is a Christian. 2 Corinthians 6:14 explains, "Do not be unequally yoked with unbelievers. For what partnership has righteousness with lawlessness?"

If you are wondering if God wants you marry someone you really like but that person does not love God, then you have your answer. God has spoken to you through his word. God will not personally tell you to do something that completely violates his word.

The second biblical quality I believe God wants your future spouse to possess is fruit bearing. Whenever there is a true conversion in someone's heart, there is also a true change in the person's life. Many times in relationships we see what we want to see rather than seeing reality.

If your boyfriend likes Christian music and prays before meals but besides that shows no fruits of the Spirit, this is not a good sign that this is the one God has for you. Again, none of us will live perfect once God makes us perfect in Christ. God justifies us when we become a Christian (declares us righteous) but he also sanctifies us (makes us holy) throughout the course of our earthly lives. You will not live a sinless life but a true Christian will be sinning less as life goes on and as they grow in Christ. Faith without works is a dead, non-saving faith (James 2:17). God saves us by grace, through faith, and not by works; but those who are truly saved will do the good works God has prepared for him or her to do (Ephesians 2:8-10).

Therefore if a guy or girl just claims to be a Christian with their lips but does not follow Christ in his or her life, this is not the one God has for you if you are following God with your life. If you just have lip service and do not have good works in your life, then perhaps you are equally yoked and you can get married. But I imagine if you have read this far into this book you have a greater passion for God than that. Trust me, God does not want you to slow down serving him because you are now attached to someone with far less passion for Christ than you. I knew my wife was the one because I knew my service for God would be enhanced, not hindered, through our union.

The third quality of someone ready to be married is a man or woman who is ready to fulfill their biblical role in the marriage. God's will for you is that your marriage would glorify him. The way a marriage glorifies God is by reflecting God accurately. The way God has ordained a marriage to reveal his truth is through giving a wife and husband different but equally important roles. This is not the book to go through all of this, but in short God wants you to marry a man or woman who is ready to be a biblical husband or wife. (Read Ephesians 5:21-33 for more on this.)

In summary, don't look to marry Jesus' twin. No one is that perfect. The person God has for you will be a real person with real flaws. But God has given us his word as a standard and a guide. When you want to know God's will for your life, including for your future marriage, you have to start by opening up the Bible, studying it, and applying it to your life.

Don't say God is not speaking to you if your Bible is closed. If you want to know the will of God, you must know the word of God. God has spoken so clearly. Therefore when the time comes to really figure out if God is revealing the person he wants you to marry, start by comparing this person to what God has already said in the Scriptures.

Reflection Questions:

1. What danger is there when we elevate the Bible over the Spirit?

2. What danger is there when we seek to hear the Holy Spirit without ever consulting the Holy Scriptures?

3. What's the difference between studying the Bible and applying the Bible? Why are both important when you have relationship questions?

4. What does the Bible say about God's desire for Christian marriages? What type of person does God want you to marry?

5. In your own words, answer this question, "How will God reveal the one to you through his word?"

Chapter 8
How Will God Reveal The One to You? (Part 2: Through His Spirit)

Hearing God's voice always starts with the Bible. If you ever "hear God" say something that contradicts Scripture, you have not actually heard God. The voice of God can be heard every time you submit to the Holy Spirit illuminating the Scriptures to your heart and mind.

While in one sense, knowing the will of God is equivalent to knowing the word of God, I believe there is another avenue of hearing God that is available to Christians. There are morally neutral choices that get set before us. Oftentimes either choice is biblical but the decision is still weighty and important, deserving of much prayer and contemplation. Relationships often fall into this category.

Marriage is good and singleness is good, but which one is right for you? Dating a Christian is good, however, what if a Christian wants to date you but you are not sure how you feel about this person? Online dating is not a sin but it does come with a variety of issues, so should you try it or not? If you are getting serious with someone but you are only slightly physically attracted rather than really attracted, should you consider marrying this person? Should you date your good friend and risk the chance of ruining a friendship if it does not work out romantically? None of these types of choices in life are answered through a clear command in the Bible. You could go either way morally.

It's in these types of relationship situations that I believe you need the Holy Spirit to give you specific directions through speaking to your heart.

Two Common Errors Regarding "Hearing the Holy Spirit"

The first error would be total dismissal of hearing God's voice personally and replacing it with sole reliance on biblical principles. Of course relying on biblical wisdom is always right, but to replace the Holy Spirit with the Bible is a huge mistake. If you never slow down to listen to God's personal words to you, you are missing out. The second error is to ignore the Bible and wisdom and equate faith with no planning, no wisdom, and total moment to moment reliance on the Holy Spirit's voice for every decision, from when to brush your teeth to who you should marry.

Personal counsel from God has zero authority compared to Scripture. To give what you feel God is saying equal value with what the Bible actually says is foolishness. Also, sometimes an over dependence on needing to hear God's personal voice about every little decision that you will ever make is actually rooted in a lack of faith rather than an abundance of faith. When you know God is sovereign and in control, this gives you peace to live your normal life without stressing about insignificant choices.

All that to say, it can be difficult to know what topics God wants to personally lead you on. Certainly he has given us a brain and as we go through the day we will literally make thousands of morally neutral decisions we don't need Bible verses to make.

As humans, sin occurs when we use a good thing in a bad way. I believe we can even use "prayer" incorrectly by trying to turn God into a rubrics cube type of God where we need to follow a perfect combination of decisions to unlock his blessings. This is not what I'm talking about when referring to hearing the voice of God and trying to know what God's will is for you. So while I don't believe you need to "hear God" about what socks to wear in the morning or how much creamer you should put in your coffee, I do believe the Holy Spirit wants to guide you through life in intimate, specific ways.

Faith can be expressed through trusting in God and not stressing the small stuff. But faith can also be expressed by slowing down enough to pray and ask God for directions on what to do. You will need to be thoughtful, biblical, and prayerful to find the right balance in your life.

How to Hear The Holy Spirit's Personal Leading to You

I'm not exactly sure what word to use here that you would be familiar with, but the Holy Spirit places "impressions" or "directions" or "discernment" on our hearts. He "gives us a word" or "leads us." When the Holy Spirit personally directs us, people describe this process differently. It usually depends on what theological background you are coming from.

I prefer to stay away from language like "God told me" or "God said to me" because this feels too close to the language of the false prophets God had rebuked because they were claiming to hear from God when in actuality they had not (Jeremiah 23:16). The personal "words" or "leading" of the Holy Spirit we get are not authoritative like the Bible.

So while I do believe Scripture supports the general principle of the Holy Spirit personally leading us in our lives, I believe it is wise to always remember we can certainly make mistakes about what God is actually saying to us. We are not infallible and therefore I believe it is wiser to say things like "I feel like God is saying to me" or "I felt like in that moment God had told me" or "I know I could be wrong, but I really feel led by the Lord to" as these phrases give room for God to move and for you as a human to make mistakes on hearing God.

My point here is really not about what words you say but what you believe in your heart. I'm sure if you combed through this book I probably used a phrase like "God said" or "God told me." Words are important, but we don't want to turn legalistic either. So yes, I believe God the Holy Spirit can lead you personally in your life, but I also believe humans can follow incorrectly. Whenever we approach God, we must always come in humility.

With semantics behind us, one of the most helpful and practical pieces of advice I've learned on "how to hear the voice of God" was from John Eldredge in his book, *Walking with God*. I would not recommend going to John Eldredge for baseline theology, but I believe there is much to learn from his relationship with Jesus and his understanding of human identity.

In the book he talks about how to hear God and get direction when you have real choices to make, "Should you go this way or that way?" He suggests you sit before the Lord in prayer and "try on" each option. To "try on" the options in a given situation means to sit before the Lord with one option and then do that again with the other option, listening to his leading as you do so. Usually you can sense which way God is leading you when you try out each option in prayerful contemplation.

So let's say you are a guy and you are trying to hear if God is giving you a "No" or a "Yes" about if you should ask a girl out on a date with you. You have already tested both options against the Scriptures and you know neither choice would violate God's written word because this girl is also a Christian and has great qualities. So in prayer you try both options out as you sit before the Lord, listening for his leading and being sensitive to what direction he's leading your tender, responsive, new heart (Ezekiel 36:26, NLT).

First you sit before the Lord with the "No, don't ask her out" option and you try to get a sense for what God might be saying. And then you sit before the Lord with the "Yes, ask her out" option and again you quiet your heart so you can hear God's leading. Often times you can get a sense of what God might be leading you to do through the impression the Holy Spirit is putting on your heart during these moments of prayer.

When I practice this tactic, I can usually get a sense for which option God is leading me to take. This method of prayer and seeking Jesus' personal leading in my life has been immensely helpful to me in my life and in my marriage.

How to Be More Confident You Are Actually Hearing God's Voice and Not Your Own

When you are praying about relationship decisions, it is crucial you are genuinely ready to obey any answer God gives you. If you know you are unwilling to accept a "No," you will not be able to fully trust when God is giving you a "Yes." You will constantly worry you are simply making his voice up in your head to get the answer you want because you know you want that answer so bad. But if you are ready to do what he says even if you don't like it, this adds to the confidence you are actually hearing God rather than your own preferences.

Again, of course there is huge room for mistakes when talking about this type of personal leading by the Holy Spirit. Of course we must continue to rely on the clarity of the Scriptures when making relationship choices. Hearing God through the impressions the Holy Spirit is putting on your heart is highly subjective and has massive room for error. It is very easy to trick yourself into hearing what you want to hear from God. So again, never make a decision without first prayerfully considering what God has already communicated in his written word.

But let's be honest, millions of morally neutral choices will come at us throughout life and especially in relationships. Do we really think God has nothing to say about these choices we need to make in our romantic lives? Why would God tell us in his word to pray about everything if God doesn't care about the things we are praying about? Surely God speaks to us personally through the intimate presence of his Holy Spirit.

I am a reformed, evangelical, theologically minded person. So I know this section can make my Calvinist, fundamental brothers and sisters nervous. If you are not biblically convinced God speaks this way, don't do it since anything not done by faith is sin (Romans 14:23). It is crucial, therefore, to first go to the word of God yourself to confirm that this category of hearing God is biblical to begin with.

While we don't have the time here to do that right now, I encourage you to study this topic for yourself. I truly believe Jesus' sheep hear his voice in deeply personal ways because the Bible points to this over and over again (John 10:27, John 8:47, Romans 8:14, Romans 12:1-2, Hebrews 3:15, Acts 13:2, Galatians 5:16, Psalm 32:8-9). I also believe in the Holy Spirit's personal leading because I have experienced it firsthand far too often for it to be coincidental nonsense. As Paul experienced in Acts 20:22-23, "And now, compelled by the Spirit, I am going to Jerusalem, not knowing what will happen to me there. [23] I only know that in every city the Holy Spirit warns me that prison and hardships are facing me."

This Bible passage gives us great balance. We will not always be able to know the answer to every decision we make. Most of the time we will not know the specifics of our future. But we do know that the Holy Spirit is speaking words of warning and counsel to us. And even though we will not always hear God's word perfectly because we are flawed, we can still be compelled by his Spirit to follow the directions he has given us.

Paul didn't know what would happen; he just knew what he had to do. Likewise, we should focus more on what God has shown us rather than worrying about what he has not yet revealed.

God Will Reveal The One to You Through the Holy Spirit Speaking to Your Heart

Perhaps the most biblical language for what we are talking about in this chapter would fall under "discernment." Hebrews 5:13-14 explains:

> ". . . for everyone who lives on milk is unskilled in the word of righteousness, since he is a child. [14] But solid food is for the mature, for those who have their powers of discernment trained by constant practice to distinguish good from evil."

When we know God's word deeply, the Holy Spirit will give us more and more insight on how to apply God's word to the varying circumstances and decisions we will experience in life and relationships. Discernment is needed to choose between good and evil. Most often God will make our decisions clear in singleness, dating, and marriage by making the path of righteousness obvious compared to the path of wickedness. When holiness and sin are the two options, it is easy to hear the Holy Spirit's leading and discernment.

However, when there is a morally neutral relationship choice to make, I still believe God is often leading us to choose one way and not the other. Perhaps sometimes he will say something like, "It doesn't matter. Either choice is fine. Do what you want. Just do it for my glory." And perhaps other times he will say, "Don't do that. Do this instead." The most important thing is that we take the time to ask God the questions we have. More often than not I believe God simply wants us to make choices that glorify him. When you know what choice will most glorify God, you know what choice God wants you to make.

When God brings the person he wants you to marry into your life, your final choice will not be accomplished through an in-depth Bible study. Yes, of course consult your Bible. But just because someone checks all the biblical boxes does not mean God is calling you to marry that person. God will confirm your choice through the impressions of the Holy Spirit on your heart.

Feeling led by God to marry someone is not the only factor you should follow in making your decision. You should be wise and listen to the counsel of those you love too. But if everyone is telling you to marry someone and you know the Bible does not condemn it, but you also feel the Holy Spirit saying, "No," then you must submit to the Spirit's leading in your life. Again, don't think you should just hear the Holy Spirit's "Yes" and marry someone even though the Bible's commands contradict this marriage choice and your friends and family are warning you not to do it.

The personal leading of the Holy Spirit is not the only way God speaks, but it is an extremely important way he speaks, especially when it comes to relationships. Getting married is a biblical option, not a biblical command. According to the Bible, marriage is for those who want to be married. Therefore it makes biblical sense that you should be led by your desires and the personal leading of the Holy Spirit when you make relationship choices because romantic relationships in general are optional. God gives us guidelines on romance and marriage, but he does not command us to be romantic and get married. Therefore you must follow the Holy Spirit's personal leading to make these personal choices.

Lastly, if for some reason you can't decipher what God the Holy Spirit is saying specifically to your heart, don't waste your day by stressing over small choices. The bigness of each choice should dictate the level of effort you put into hearing God's voice about it. If you don't feel led by God one way or the other, do what you feel will most glorify him. Do what is most biblical. Do what is wisest. And do what brings you the most enjoyment (without sinning). God is not opposed to happiness. He is opposed to seeking happiness in sinful ways.

Just don't miss out on the intimate leading of the Holy Spirit by assuming he has nothing to say to you personally about your relationships and your future marriage. Prayer is meant to be a conversation and a conversation includes talking and listening. Those who hear God are those who regularly quiet their hearts to listen to what God is saying.

Reflection Questions:

1. What are your general thoughts about this chapter? Do you believe in the "personal leading of the Holy Spirit" as described in this chapter? Why or why not?

2. Why is it important to never give "hearing God in my heart" the same authority as God's written word?

3. Why is it so important to not only make sure a relationship is biblical but to also make sure it is the right relationship for you? In other words, will God ever make you marry someone you don't want to marry? Explain.

4. What are some ways you can try to make sure you are not just making God's voice up in your head so you can hear what you want about a relationship?

5. In your own words, answer this question, "How will God reveal the one to you through the personal leading of the Holy Spirit?"

Chapter 9
How Will God Reveal The One to You? (Part 3: Through Your Circumstances)

So far we have learned that God will reveal what he wants you to do in relationships through his word and also through the personal leading of the Holy Spirit. These are not the only ways God speaks. Because God is in sovereign control of the world and each of our individual lives, we can also look at the circumstances we experience to learn what God is saying to us.

Our present circumstances provide us with a treasure chest of information about God's will for our lives right now. Projecting where God wants you to be in the future is much more challenging. But whenever you have a question about the present, you can always hear God's answer through your present reality.

God's Sovereign Will (Not Prescribed Will) Always Happens, Therefore Whatever Happens Is God's Sovereign Will

This idea sounds so obvious it almost feels not worth mentioning. But stating the obvious about God speaking through our circumstances is necessary because we live in an age where postmodernism is embraced and absolute truth is despised. We have to be careful we do not get sucked into the guru nonsense of our era.

In other words, your reality is not whatever you believe it to be. Your reality is reality whether you accept it as reality or not. Your truth and my truth can't both be right if they are different. You can't speak things into existence. Absolute truth exists whether you believe it or not. God really is in control.

So why am I saying this in a book about how God will reveal the one to you? It's important to fully accept that God is in control of our world in every way because this allows us to answer questions we have about what God is saying "yes" or "no" to in our lives right now. For example:

- If you are hearing God say "date Laura" but Laura has rejected your last ten invitations and told you she will call the police next time you call her, you are not hearing God correctly. God is speaking through the circumstances of this relationship.

- If you hear God say, "Quit your job because that book you wrote is about to be a bestseller in one week" but you've been trying to pitch it to publishers for years and no one has even seemed remotely interested, God is probably not telling you to quit your job. God's voice can be clearly heard in the absence of interest this book is generating in reality.

- If you are wondering if God wants you to date William but then William starts dating Amber, God is speaking to you about your relationship with William through William's relationship with Amber.

- If you are wondering if you should buy that house but then someone else buys it, you don't have to sit around wondering if you should still put an offer in. God has spoken.

All of these examples are limited to the present. Maybe Laura will change her mind one day. Maybe the book deal will come. Maybe William and Amber will breakup and then you and William might start dating. Perhaps the buyer will fall through and the house will come back on the market in a few weeks.

Right now, however, in each of those situations God has spoken because God speaks through our circumstances. Throughout the Bible God instructs his people to learn how to read the times, to look at the circumstances and rightly judge what God is obviously doing or not doing. For example, in Luke 12:54-56 Jesus said to the crowd:

> "When you see a cloud rising in the west, you say at once, 'A shower is coming.' And so it happens. [55] And when you see the south wind blowing, you say, 'There will be scorching heat,' and it happens. [56] You hypocrites! You know how to interpret the appearance of earth and sky, but why do you not know how to interpret the present time?"

Jesus is clearly not talking about relationships and marriage here. He's talking about the coming of the gospel. However, the principle certainly relates to knowing God's will in general. If you want to know what God is doing right now, all you need to do is look at what is happening right now. Sometimes we overcomplicate our search to know God's will about our singleness, dating, and future marriage because we refuse to just look at the actual details of our lives and relationships.

In Matthew 16:3-4 Jesus also said, "You know how to interpret the appearance of the sky, but you cannot interpret the signs of the times. An evil and adulterous generation seeks for a sign, but no sign will be given to it except the sign of Jonah." Again, Jesus is referring to the gospel. The sign of Jonah is Jesus being in the tomb and rising after three days just as Jonah was in the belly of the fish for three days but then came out. We can see Jesus' frustration with people who want a miraculous sign while the facts of real life are staring them right in the face. Often times we want answers about our relationships and futures while God has given us all the answers we need right in our present.

In the Bible God warns his people not to put up with false prophets. But how are the people to know what prophets are true and which are false? In Deuteronomy 18:21-22 God gave the people some very practical counsel on how to decipher between true prophecy and false words from God:

> "And if you say in your heart, 'How may we know the word that the Lord has not spoken?'— 22 when a prophet speaks in the name of the Lord, if the word does not come to pass or come true, that is a word that the Lord has not spoken; the prophet has spoken it presumptuously. You need not be afraid of him."

God makes it real simple for the people, "If reality matches the prophesy, the prophesy was in alignment with my will. If the prophesy doesn't happen in reality, that prophet did not hear my voice."

So if you want to know the will of God for your singleness, dating, and marriage right now in this present season, sometimes all you need to do is look around. He is speaking through the events in our lives all the time. To be balanced, *only* looking at the circumstances of your life is not sufficient because most of our questions have to do with the future. As we all know, our present can change in a moment.

What Your Circumstances Do Not Mean

It's important to take a step back for a moment and clarify the limits this method has. Your circumstances cannot tell you everything and you can easily misinterpret them to mean things they do not mean. For example, it would be unbiblical to interpret "good" circumstances with "God loves me" and "bad" circumstances with "God hates me."

Your subjective feelings about God's feelings towards you should be guided by the objective facts God has revealed in Scripture rather than the ever-changing circumstances of your life. When we fail to rely on God's word as the guide to interpreting our circumstances, we can trick ourselves into thinking God is pleased with our sinfulness and displeased with our service. Why? Because without the Bible we can interpret our lives however we want. And since we are flawed we will certainly interpret things wrong.

Again, the Bible helps us interpret our reality. For example, just because you are sick does not mean God no longer loves you. The Bible says God shows his love by glorifying himself through our lives, and sometimes that means God shows his love not by sparing us of trials but by glorifying himself through our lives as we walk with him through those trials (John 11:1-6).

So we must be cautious when using our circumstances to hear the voice of God. Again, it is best to use this method of hearing God's voice when our questions are about the present. If you are asking, "Should I move to Texas to be with my girlfriend?" but then your girlfriend breaks up with you, God has spoken a "No" on that question through these circumstances. But if you are asking this question and your girlfriend is encouraging you to come, but you still have inner concerns about the move, you need more than your present circumstances to know God's will for you.

This is why to hear the voice of God clearly, we must combine all three of the ways God speaks. In his book, *Hearing God*, when Dallas Willard was writing about the "three lights" by which we can hear the voice of God, he explains the importance of using all three together:

> "These are circumstances, impressions of the Spirit, and passages from the Bible. When these three things point in the same direction . . . we [can] be sure the direction they point is the one God intends for us."

When you combine God's word with what you feel the Holy Spirit is saying and with what the reality of the relationship looks like, you are giving yourself the best possible opportunity to clearly hear what God is saying to you about this relationship. When I was weighing through my decision to ask Bethany to marry me, I had to make sure it checked out biblically. I then wanted to make sure I felt peace in my own heart with God about it. But I also had to live in reality and ask Bethany to marry me and her "Yes" was the final confirmation I needed.

One great biblical example of how these three means of knowing God's will can work together is in the account of Saul wandering into a cave in which David was hiding. Saul was sinfully hunting David even though David had done nothing to deserve this. When Saul entered the cave, David's men interpreted this circumstance different than David because they were not walking with God and did not know God's commands like David. 1 Samuel 24:4-7 states:

> "And the men of David said to him, 'Here is the day of which the LORD said to you, 'Behold, I will give your enemy into your hand, and you shall do to him as it shall seem good to you.'' Then David arose and stealthily cut off a corner of Saul's robe. [5] And afterward David's heart struck him, because he had cut off a corner of Saul's robe. [6] He said to his men, 'The LORD forbid that I should do this thing to my lord, the LORD's anointed, to put out my hand against him, seeing he is the LORD's anointed.' [7] So David persuaded his men with these words and did not permit them to attack Saul. And Saul rose up and left the cave and went on his way."

If David was only looking at the circumstances he would have sinned. His men interpreted this event very differently because they were not being balanced like David. They were only looking at the present circumstances. David knew God's law and was filled with God's Spirit; therefore, he did not let an exciting circumstance overwhelm him and cause him to sin. Later David knew God had truly given him the kingdom and taken it from Saul when it all happened in a way where David did not need to violate God's commands. David followed God's prescribed will and allowed God to fulfill God's sovereign will.

When we seek to follow God's will for our lives, we must do the same as David did. To have the best chance of doing what God wants, when God wants, and in the way God wants, we must depend on God's word and his Spirit inside of us so we can rightly interpret the circumstances of our lives and relationships.

God Will Reveal The One to You Through the Circumstances of the Relationship

I often get comments on my YouTube channel or on ApplyGodsWord.com from people who want to know what God is saying to them about a certain relationship. Usually this person really likes someone a lot, they tell me the details of their situation, and then they ask me what God's will is.

I obviously start by telling them that I have no idea what God's will is for them. However, often times I am able to give them a very firm idea of what I believe God's will is for them when the circumstances of their relationship with someone are very clear and obvious. Below is not an uncommon example of the comments and questions that often come in:

> "Dear Mark, I really need your advice. I have been dating this guy for three years and I truly love him.

All of a sudden he broke up with me and he won't give me another chance. Every time we talk he keeps telling me he does not love me enough to marry me so he does not want to date anymore. I just don't know what to do. I really love him and want to be with him. What is God's will here? What is God telling me to do?"

While my heart certainly breaks for anyone going through such relationship heartache, her question is not hard to answer. I don't know what will happen in the future. Maybe one day the guy's feelings will change and they will have a great marriage. All I know is that this guy said he does not want to be with her anymore. God is speaking through these details of her life. We can say with confidence that it is not God's will for these two to be together in a relationship right now because the guy clearly said he does not want to be in a relationship with her right now. God has spoken.

It seems obvious to us reading her words, but that's because we are not emotionally involved like her. When you want something so bad, it can be easy to allow your hope to cloud your vision of reality as it really is. When we cling to what we want rather than to what we actually have in life, we are treading on dangerous ground and getting nearer and nearer to a state of delusion. When you start closing your eyes to what is actually happening, oftentimes it is like closing your ears to the voice of God.

One common mistake I often see is that people dream so long about being with someone before making a move to actually be with this person, they build up a false reality in their head. They start thinking about marriage before even talking to the person they are dreaming about. This type of thinking is not helpful because it causes you to focus too much on your desires and imagined relationship rather than on what is actually happening between you and this person.

For example, if you are wondering if God wants you to date someone who does not want to date you, you don't need to ask God about this anymore. No, God does not want you to date that person. If God wanted you to date that person, that person would also want to date you. Or if someone is ignoring your calls, you don't have to ask God what this means. It means that person does not want to talk with you and you need to respect their freedom to make that choice. If a guy asks you on a date, this means he likes you. Again, I know all this seems painfully obvious but sometimes we overlook real life because we live too much in our heads.

Many of us think singleness, dating, and finding your future spouse would be a lot easier if we could all just read each other's minds and hearts. We just wish we could know what the other person is thinking. But this is not how God has made us. We can't truly know someone's thoughts, feelings, or motives. However, people's actions are a reflection of their thoughts, feelings, and motives. While we cannot know for certain the inner workings of someone just because we can see their actions, what they do does give us some glimpses into how they might be feelings (key word "might"). You will not be able to *prove* anything, but you can gather some *evidence* about someone's feelings towards you by observing their actions towards you.

Jesus said you shall know them by their fruit (Matthew 7:16). In context Jesus was not talking about relationships and dating. He was talking about how you can know a true Christian from a false Christian. Jesus meant that we cannot know someone's heart. Man can only look at the outward appearance of things and only God knows the heart (1 Samuel 16:7). But humans can look at the actions of people's lives and have a decent understanding of what is going on in their hearts because the inner man controls the outer life. We cannot see someone's roots. Only God can see below the surface. We can, however, see the fruit someone is producing in their life. You can know the health of the tree by looking at the fruit it is bearing.

We can take that principle and apply it to this question of "How can you know if someone likes you or not?" We can't truly know the thoughts and feelings of someone else's heart. Besides just having an open conversation, all we can do is look at the actions of their lives to see what we can learn about their feelings. This can certainly be dangerous because we can often read into things that really don't mean anything. We are told to not judge the heart of someone else because we often make assumptions based on our hopes rather than evidence. With that said, relationships can be complicated and sometimes it helps to know what God is saying by taking a closer look at the reality of the relationship and what the other person is doing.

So when God brings the person he wants you to marry into your life, he or she will meet certain requirements found in the Bible. You will feel good about marrying him or her. But there will also be very obvious circumstances in your life to confirm what you feel. When God reveals your future spouse to you, the circumstances of your relationship will be clear. The two of you will love each other, you will want to be married, and the other common-sense factors will be in place.

Reflection Questions:

1. Do you believe God speaks through circumstances? Why or why not?

2. Read 1 Samuel 24:4-7. Why was David able to better interpret the circumstances compared to his men?

3. What's the danger in relationships when we let our hopes skew our ability to look at reality?

4. It has been said by millions of mothers throughout history, "Actions speak louder than words." How does this advice help you make decisions in relationships?

5. In your own words, answer this question, "How will God reveal the one to you through the circumstances in your life?"

Chapter 10
What Should You Do If You Are Not Sure If God Is Revealing The One to You?

As we wrap up this discussion on how to know God's will for your future marriage, we must acknowledge that sometimes, despite our best efforts and methods, we can find it difficult to hear what God is saying to do. So what should you do when you cannot hear the voice of God? What should you do when you don't have clarity on his will for you and your relationship with someone from the opposite sex?

In this chapter I will give you three biblical questions you can ask yourself when you are not sure what God's will is for you. These can be asked anytime you are not sure what to do, but they can be especially helpful when you have questions about your singleness, dating, and future marriage. The three questions are:

1. What choice will be most glorifying and pleasing to God?
2. What choice is the wisest and aligns best with Scripture?
3. What choice would bring me the most personal satisfaction?

When you don't have a specific Bible verse or biblical truth to instruct you, when you don't feel the Holy Spirit leading you one way or the other, and when the circumstances are not clearly pointing you in a certain direction, answering these three questions may help you decide what you should do.

What Choice Would Be Most Glorifying to God?

When in doubt about the voice of God, you should examine your motives. Choose the decision that is supported by your best, most Christlike motive.

When your motive is to glorify God, you always make the correct choice spiritually. Sure, sometimes we can be well intentioned but make unwise practical choices that don't turn out the way we wanted in regards to our earthly circumstances. But when your desire is to please God, you are on the correct path to pleasing God.

Glorifying God is often times less about what you do and more about how you do it. Putting God first is not about putting God in the first box, putting your marriage in the second box, putting your children in the third box, putting your career in the fourth box, and so on. God never wants to be in a box. Rather, he wants to consume every box you have in life. Putting God first in your life occurs when you seek to glorify God in your search for a spouse, in your marriage, in your parenting, in your career, and so on.

You may not always know what God wants you to do in life and relationships. But sometimes we get so confused because we should be focusing less on the "what" and more on the "how." How are you walking through singleness? How are you dating? How are you searching for your future spouse? You can do all of these things in a sinful way or a glorifying way. Following God's will for your life is more about you living your life in a Christlike way rather than you making the "right" decision about everything that ever comes your way, "Should I go out tonight? Should I friend request this girl on social media that I like at church? Should I sit next to her at church?" These are less important decisions compared to your decision to do everything in a wholesome, Christlike way.

> "And whatever you do, in word or deed, do everything in the name of the Lord Jesus, giving thanks to God the Father through him." (Colossians 3:17)

> "So, whether you eat or drink, or whatever you do, do all to the glory of God." (1 Corinthians 10:31)

Many times Christians complain about what is not in the Bible. They wish that God the Holy Spirit would have directed the Apostle Peter to write a chapter with the 100 steps to take to meet, date, and marry your future spouse. The word of God does not cover every topic we will deal with in life. It does, however, have all the information we need to live a glorifying life.

Whatever God has included in the Scriptures is exactly what we need. So if God has not given us a dating blueprint, for example, it means God does not require us all to follow a one-size-fits-all dating approach. Rather than give us formulas and steps to follow in relationships, God has given us principles and truths to live by. If God is not giving you the steps to take, perhaps he is saying it doesn't matter what step you take compared to "how" you take that step. When you do things for the glory of God, you are doing the right thing.

Therefore, next time you are not sure what God's will is for you, just ask yourself, "What would bring God the most glory? What decision will magnify him the most and reveal Jesus the most to those in my circle of influence?" God does not always give us the steps to take, but he has told us he always wants us to glorify him in everything we do.

(For more on this topic, you may enjoy my other book, *Intertwined: Our Happiness Is Tied to God's Glory*.)

What Choice Is the Wisest and Best Aligns With the Bible?

Secondly, God is a God of order and wisdom. So when you don't know what to do and you are having difficulty making a decision, you will make far less mistakes by choosing the way of wisdom and practicality. Do what makes the most sense if you don't feel God leading you one way or the other.

It's important to note, however, that God does sometimes lead us to make decisions based more on faith than wisdom, not that these two are opposed at all. Sometimes he even asks us to make "unwise" (never sinful) decisions.

It was unwise of Gideon to cut the fighting men from 22,000 to 300 (Judges 7). It was unwise of Moses to lead a massive group of people full of women, children, and untrained men out from under the rule of Pharaoh and his highly trained army (Exodus 14). It was unwise of Joseph to marry his already pregnant fiancé (Matthew 1:18-25). In each of these cases God asked those involved to step out in faith and trust him.

It's important to emphasize, however, that in each of these unwise decisions, God gave those involved an abundance of confirmation. God gave Gideon a clear sign to use to cut the number of men down to just 300 (Judges 7:4-8). God had continually appeared to Moses in fantastic ways before asking him to make such a huge step of faith (read the book of Exodus). And an angel appeared to Joseph to let him know Marry was not fooling around but had a child conceived by the Holy Spirit (Matthew 1:18-25).

Therefore, I believe a general principle in Scripture is that the greater the step of faith God asks you to take the greater the confirmation he will supply. By "confirmation" I simply mean a different piece of evidence that is pointing to the same conclusion as other pieces of evidence. If you feel God is saying he wants you to step out in faith and do something that most people would consider "unwise," you should be sure to get God's confirmation on it.

God will never tell you to do something wild through a voice in your head and then give you no other clear signs to confirm that thought was from him. Whatever step of faith you feel God may lead you to take, you should always be able to justify it with biblical wisdom even if the choice will not be the wisest financial, practical, or relational decision. And if the decision before you would lead to sin, you can be certain God is not telling you to make that decision.

With all that said, normally God speaks to us through the wisdom he provides in Scripture. Making wise, practical decisions is not a lack of faith. There are a lot of poor teachings out there that make people feel a life of faith is a life that shuns wisdom and is run by spur of the moment decisions and "walking by the Spirit." Yes, Christians must walk by the Spirit, but the Holy Spirit inspired the Holy Scriptures, therefore we should expect a Holy Spirit-led-life to also be a Bible-based-life. When we trust God he leads us to follow his word.

> "If any of you lacks wisdom, let him ask God, who gives generously to all without reproach, and it will be given him." (James 1:5)

"But be doers of the word, and not hearers only, deceiving yourselves. [23] For if anyone is a hearer of the word and not a doer, he is like a man who looks intently at his natural face in a mirror. [24] For he looks at himself and goes away and at once forgets what he was like. [25] But the one who looks into the perfect law, the law of liberty, and perseveres, being no hearer who forgets but a doer who acts, he will be blessed in his doing." (James 1:22-25)

When you are unsure of what to do in life and in your relationships, do what is wisest. Don't marry a man who has no source of income. Don't date a girl who consistently cheats on all her boyfriends. Don't pay for a plane ticket for someone halfway across the world because they showed interest in you online. If you don't know what to do, just ask yourself, "What's the wisest, most mature choice I can make?"

What Choice Corresponds With Your Desires the Most?

I put this question last because here is where I know I can be taken out of context very easily. I'm not saying in this section that you should do whatever you want because God just wants you to be happy. But I do believe God wants you to do things that you enjoy. I believe God often speaks through our desires. If you have a good, Christ honoring desire to do something, it's very likely God put it there himself.

Sometimes we overcomplicate choices in singleness, dating, and in Christian relationships by thinking God usually tells us to do things we do not want to do. When sin is not in the equation and multiple options are before you, I believe God is usually saying, "Just do what you enjoy!" If you would rather spend more time with Matthew even though your friends are pressuring you to spend more time with Jake, pray about it to see if you are missing something. But if you still don't know what to do, just spend more time with Matthew because that's what you want to do.

Paul proclaimed, "Woe to me if I do not preach the gospel!" (1 Corinthians 9:16). Paul was called to preach, but certainly Paul also knew his calling because he loved to preach. Likewise, God often leads us down the paths that he wants us to take by placing a desire on our hearts.

So when you don't know what to do in singleness, in dating, or in your pursuit of your future marriage, certainly do what is biblical and wise. However, you must also not forget the desires God has placed on your heart. God often leads us down the paths he wants by placing those passions on our hearts. When God reveals the one, you will *want* to date and then marry him or her.

We tend to make this topic of "knowing God's will" very confusing and stressful. But there truly is no reason to stress. Even if you do not hear the voice of God accurately or you are unsure if you did the exact right thing, you can take comfort in the sovereignty of God. Listen to hear his voice but trust him even when you don't. While we certainly can bring harm to ourselves and others if we never slow down and listen for God's leading, God is more than able to turn anything for his glory. We don't need to know everything when we know he knows everything. We can rest in his ability to be God.

When It's Time for God to Reveal The One to You, You Will Just Know

In closing, if you are still unsure if God has revealed the one to you, don't get married. Feel free to keep building a friendship or a dating relationship when you are unsure of your future with someone. That's the point of Christian dating – to figure out if two people want to get married or not. If you are unsure, don't get married.

Love is always a risk. You can't ever really know how your future marriage will turn out. So I'm not saying you must know your whole future before you say "I do" at the wedding altar. What I am saying is that you never want to marry someone if you are not sure God wants you to marry that person.

When you feel the peace of God confirming that he does want you to marry this person, this peace is not a promise that your future marriage will be perfect. God might tell you to marry someone and that marriage might be very difficult. Every marriage has its ups and downs. But unlike friendship and dating, God has called Christians to make a lifelong commitment in marriage. What God has joined together, man should not separate (Mark 10:9). Therefore choosing to marry someone is one of the biggest decisions you will ever make.

Now for the vaguest and perhaps most unhelpful (or most helpful, depending on how you look at) advice: When you meet the one God wants you to marry, you will just know. People say this all the time and it makes no sense until you experience it for yourself. But for me and for everyone else

I've talked to about this subject, this statement, "You will just know," is true when it comes to answering the question, "How does God let you know that you've found the right person?"

Seek God, love God, follow God, obey God, trust God, and he will make it clear who he wants you to marry. You won't know until it's time. Therefore, just follow him and enjoy the ride. He's training you right now for what's ahead.

Reflection Questions:

1. Should we expect to always know God's will for our lives and relationships? Explain.

2. Do you believe it is a good rule to rely on wisdom when you do not sense God's leading one way or the other? Explain.

3. Do you believe it is okay to make choices based on your personal desires? Explain.

4. What's the purpose of Christian dating? Should you ever marry someone if you have doubts? Explain.

5. What are your thoughts about the common advice of, "When you meet the one, you will just know."? Do you find this helpful or unhelpful? Explain.

Chapter 11
Does God Ever Speak Through Dreams and "Prophetic Words" About Relationships?

Many people ask me about interpreting dreams from God, specifically when it comes to dreams about dating and their future marriage. Another common question that comes in surprisingly often is about prophesy and relationships.

For example, I remember one guy wrote in and reported someone "prophesied over" him and told him that they "saw" him surrounded by a woman and lots of children." The only problem is that this guy was very content in his singleness and did not want to get married or have kids.

So what do you do when something like this happens to you? How much weight should you give to dreams you have about dating, dreams you have about your future marriage, and "prophesies" that people speak over you about your relationship future?

God Can Do Whatever He Wants

As I'm sure you've figured out by now, I admittedly come from a more reformed perspective. So while I will lean differently than those with a more liberal view on Scripture and the gifts of the Spirit, I am still a continuationist and not a cessationist.

I also do not want to put God in a box and say he can and cannot speak in certain ways. So I believe God can give you a dream that actually means something and I believe God can give some glimpse of something about your future as a way to warn or help you. However, I don't believe this normally happens and if it does occur I believe there will also be certain qualifiers around all this, which we will discuss shortly.

I appreciate John Piper's insight found in his article titled *The New Testament Gift of Prophecy*. He explains that there is perfect prophecy that is recorded in Scripture. There is also false prophecy that totally contradicts Scripture and thus is not from God. But there is a third type of prophecy we experience today where we as Christians must sift through the biblical and unbiblical words of the person speaking. Piper states:

> "Prophecy in this 'third category' (the New Testament gift of prophecy) is a regulated message or report in human words usually made to the gathered believers based on a spontaneous, personal revelation from the Holy Spirit for the purpose of edification, encouragement, consolation, conviction or guidance but not necessarily free from a mixture of human error, and thus needing assessment on the basis of the apostolic (Biblical) teaching and mature spiritual wisdom."

The above type of prophecy is what I believe is most biblical in this season of God's redemptive history. The reason I don't believe God usually leads us anymore through dreams and someone's prophetic words over us is because we live in a time where we have God's word. The Holy Spirit wrote his words in the Bible for a reason. Therefore I believe dreams and supernatural events are more likely to occur in places where Christianity is new and the Bible is not as available.

There Are Many False Prophets, Thus There Are Many False Prophesies

If someone "spoke prophetic words over you" and told you something about your future marriage, you should be able to test what they said against the Scriptures. If anyone proclaims something that contradicts the word of God, you know that word was not from God.

Whenever someone in the Bible was given a dream or a prophetic message, the interpretation was not hidden for long. God always provided a clear interpretation. The same is true when people spoke in tongues. There was always to be someone there who could interpret what was being said in tongues, otherwise the person should not have been speaking in tongues publicly because it was not helping those who heard it because no one was there to interpret (1 Corinthians 14:27-28).

I believe these same principles should guide our questions about dreams and words from a prophet. If it's confusing, it's probably not God, "For God is not a God of confusion but of peace" (1 Corinthians 14:33).

There are many people who make prophesies and talk about their dreams because they want to be exalted amongst the people. The Bible says there are many false prophets and we should not believe everything someone says just because they claim to be a prophet:

> "Beloved, do not believe every spirit, but test the spirits to see whether they are from God, for many false prophets have gone out into the world." (1 John 4:1)

"For such men are false apostles, deceitful workmen, disguising themselves as apostles of Christ. And no wonder, for even Satan disguises himself as an angel of light. So it is no surprise if his servants, also, disguise themselves as servants of righteousness. Their end will correspond to their deeds." (2 Corinthians 11:13-15)

The surest test of a true prophet is if what they say aligns with what God has already clearly said in his word. There will never be "new" revelations. The second way to test a prophecy is to simply see if it occurs. If it does not happen, it was not from God. When God proclaims something, it always happens (Deuteronomy 18:21-22).

This is why you should not put too much stock in a prophetic word about your future. If it happens, it happens. If not, it didn't happen. Reality is reality (profound, I know). When God gave us prophesies about the gospel and the coming of Christ, it was to show the greatness of God and to show he is in control. I think false prophets have the same motive; they want to be exalted and try to take control of people by telling them their futures. (False prophets are not really telling them the future. They are just guessing.)

The problem is when people value a "prophetic word" so much they start trying to make that word come true. Rather than the prophecy revealing their future, now this prophecy starts controlling their future. This is not right and it is a form of manipulation on the part of the prophet and a sign of immaturity by the person listening to this false prophet.

Never Try to Fulfill a Prophesy

One of the biggest mistakes I see people make when it comes to prophesy and Christian relationships is when someone feels the need to fulfill the prophesy that was spoken over them. That is definitely an unbiblical approach to how to use true prophesy from God. For example, if someone said to you, "You will marry someone with blond hair" and then you never date anyone other than people with blond hair, this is really crazy. Don't do that.

If God really said something to you through someone else or in a dream, it is not your job to make that happen. It will happen without you trying to make it happen if God actually is behind it. As I mentioned at the beginning of this chapter, recently I talked to a guy who said that someone spoke words of prophesy over him and said he was going to get married and have a family. The problem is the man had all the signs of being called to singleness. He didn't want to be married and he didn't want to have children.

You can see why this man was confused. I told the man the most logical explanation is that this person was not speaking on God's behalf. God will not tell someone his plans for your future while not revealing those plans to you. God doesn't control your life through the words of others. That's what cult leaders and false prophets try to do. They try to claim God told them something about you but in reality they just made it up and want you to try to fulfill this fake prophesy so you will actually be obeying their voice, not God's voice.

Personally I don't believe God speaks words about your future through other people very often. Again, I'm not saying God never does this or can't do this. But to me it does not pass the biblical test of regularly occurring in Scripture for all Christians and being a command to practice for all Christians. Prayer, Bible reading, listening for the Holy Spirit to lead you in your heart, following the counsel of trusted Christian brothers and sisters – these are things we can clearly see in Scripture and we are commanded to practice these things.

I'm cautious of making supernatural events in the Bible things all Christians should regularly expect to experience in life. I don't discount these supernatural dreams, visions, and prophesies in Scripture, I just don't believe the Bible says these will be a part of every Christians' life like the normal means of grace are (Bible, prayer, fellowship, etc.).

Don't Look for Supernatural Confirmation When You Need to Make a Simple Decision Already Explained in God's Word

Yes, Mary, Elizabeth, their husbands, and many others like them in the Bible experienced God's leading through dreams, visions, and angelic encounters. But they were also experiencing once-in-an-eternity kind of events. For example, when Mary and Joseph got a supernatural word from God, God himself was going to be born through a virgin birth. They needed a supernatural confirmation to authenticate this supernatural experience. Without this no one would believe Mary was telling the truth of how she got pregnant.

You wondering if you should date someone is not the same thing. You don't need a supernatural confirmation to make a very natural decision. God doesn't need to send an angel to you in a dream when you are risking nothing for him and just simply have a question about a relationship.

Just read your Bible and obey what it says. If you are not breaking a command in Scripture and you feel in your spirit God is not saying, "No," then just go on a date. God often reveals his truth through the circumstances of life. When the relationship does not work out or you know you don't like that person or that person does not like you, God has spoken. If it works out, you both are Christians, and you both want to keep dating, God has spoken. It's not normal and it should not be expected to get a dream or a prophetic word about everything.

When you need the grand signs to make simple decisions, this is actually a lack of faith, not an expression of faith. When you see how things will turn out, the need for faith is gone. Faith is believing in what you cannot see (Hebrews 11:1). If God supernaturally confirms everything about your future marriage before it happens then he is taking the need for faith away from you. God wants us to have faith in him, therefore he will not give you a dream or signs in the sky every time you have a relationship question.

When we want God to tell us everything about our future before it happens, we are looking for a fortune teller not a prophet. A prophet will help you apply biblical truth to modern times. A fortune teller tells you what you want to hear so you will give them money. I'm not trying to be offensive. I'm not trying to put down any Christians who have a different view than me. I just see so many young people being led astray and taught wild things about dreams and interpretations by people who don't know the Bible.

God has spoken! He gave his words to you in writing. It must be odd for God to look down on so many of us groping around in the night looking for the meaning of a dream we just had. He must raise an eyebrow now and then as we go up during the altar call at church and ask someone about our future. I imagine him saying, "I told them what I want them to do in writing and I am available to speak anytime in prayer. Why are they examining dreams when they haven't read their Bibles and why are they asking strangers about what will happen in their futures?"

My Opinion on the Use of Dreams

Now what I am going to do is just give you my opinion. I don't have Bible verses to back this up, but I'm just going to apply logic to this question. So what can we learn from our dreams about relationships?

When my 5-year-old son has a bad dream, I ask him to tell me what happened. Usually his dream is directly related to something he watched or to something he experienced in his life recently. Since he was thinking about something recently when he was awake, his brain created a dream about it. This is usually the case for all of us.

When we go to sleep, our brains and imaginations keep working. They use the thoughts and materials that are around to construct the dreams that we experience. So if you have been having lots of thoughts about Jason when you are awake, it's not surprising that you are now having dreams about Jason when you are asleep. If you have been thinking about your ex-girlfriend when you are awake, it's natural to have a dream about your ex-girlfriend when you are asleep.

When you have thoughts about being with someone in a relationship, do you believe your thought is a sign God is telling you he wants you to marry that person? Probably not. Why? Because you know you just made that thought up yourself. Most times this should be the approach we have with our dreams. We should not assume God is sending us messages through our dreams when in reality our dreams are just a natural biological reaction to the types of thoughts and feelings we have been having lately.

Lots of times dreams are just weird and should not be examined. Every now and then, however, it is helpful to examine the types of dreams you have been having. I don't believe it is wise to look for symbolic meaning about every detail in the dream like Daniel did with the statue in King Nebuchadnezzar's dream (Daniel 2). When Daniel did this, he was not grasping at straws or just guessing. God gave him a clear, unmistakable revelation about this dream's meaning. If you don't have a clear, supernatural revelation from God then don't try to do what Daniel did. But you might find it helpful to examine your dreams in general.

So if my son has a dream about a bear chasing him in the night, I'm not going to ask him, "Well what do you think the bear means? What does the night mean? And what color socks did you have on in the dream?" But I can use this dream to make a decision that he is not ready to watch nature shows with me anymore. If we just streamed a video last night about bears hunting prey, I can see from my son's dream he should not watch these shows yet.

I remember when I was in high school I really liked this girl and had all the typical teenage thoughts about marrying her one day. So when it didn't work out with her I was very sad for a season. But in time God began to help me move on. One night I had a dream where I was at this girls wedding and something went wrong but I helped fix the problem. Throughout the dream I had a feeling of happiness for her and her husband.

Now, it would be easy to read into every detail of this dream and wonder what it all meant. I never became friends with this girl after that dream and I did not attend her wedding. I was not a part of her life at all. And I did not feel God used this dream to say, "She's not the one." I was still young and had no idea what God would do in my life at that time. But the feeling I had in that dream gave me some good general information about what God was doing in my life. When I woke up, I felt like God had shown me I was making progress in my heart because I was happy for her in that dream.

This is not a supernatural event in my opinion. My dream was just a natural reaction to the feelings that were inside of me. God had changed my heart towards her, therefore my brain created a dream that reflected my new feelings about her. I used to have thoughts and feelings about liking her. Once those feelings changed in me, I then I had this dream about being happy for her marriage to someone else. In my opinion, the dream was a reflection of my thoughts and feelings. I'm open to being wrong. Maybe God will tell me once I go to heaven that dream was supernatural. But either way I know God was healing my heart during that time regardless of why I had that dream.

I also remember having a dream about my wife liking me at a time in our lives when we were still just friends and had not started dating yet. In the dream there were all these guys who wanted to dance with her at a wedding we were all attending. But she was saying no to all of them and waiting for me to dance with her. Again, it would have been easy to read into that dream and say this was a sign from God that we would be together. But guess what? I really liked her at that point and really wanted her to like me too. So it's not surprising that I had a dream reflecting my emotions at that time in my life. Perhaps I am wrong and this was from God. But either way that dream confirmed that I liked her more than as just a friend.

So my main point is that dreams can sometimes be used to give us clues to our own thoughts and feelings. I don't think it should be expected that dreams will be used to tell us about our future. But I think they can usually be used to tell us something about our present. Your thoughts and feelings can be revealed in what type of dreams you are having.

If you are having lots of dreams about Jerome, it could be God sending you a supernatural message. But it's probably not. You are probably having lots of dreams about Jerome because you have been thinking about Jerome and have feelings for him. If you have a dream about a baby with blue eyes and red hair, this could be a sign from God Almighty that you will have a child who looks just like that because you are going to marry someone with Irish heritage. Or it could be that you have been thinking and praying about having a family one day and this was just the picture your brain dreamed up because you have been thinking about babies so much.

So most times I would not look into your dreams too much. Sometimes I would examine your dreams too see what general things you can learn about your thoughts and emotions. But you should always be praying and reading your Bible so you know for certain what God wants you to do in life, including in your Christian relationships.

Reflection Questions:

1. Do you believe God speaks through dreams and words of prophesy from other people? Why or why not?

2. Why should we be cautious when looking at our dreams and listening to other people's "prophetic words" about our relationships?

3. Why do dreams naturally occur and how can the biological side of dreams help us learn information about ourselves?

4. If a "prophetic word" cannot be confirmed as true or not by Scripture, what is the only other test we can use to make sure this is really from God or not?

5. What is the danger of trying to fulfill a dream or a "prophetic word" someone spoke to you about your future relationship?

Chapter 12
How Can You Overcome the Fear of the Unknowns and Move Forward Towards Your Future Marriage?

Anxiety, fear of making the wrong choice, and a continued desire for all the unknowns to be made clear are common feelings in Christian singles who desire to be married one day. How will I know when God wants me to act? How will I know if God wants me to just stay put and not act? How will I know when God reveals "the one" to me?

The list of questions and concerns can be endless. These types of questions are good to ask. Singleness can be a very confusing and difficult season for some people. But throughout the Scriptures we are told not to worry, to not be anxious, and to trust God at all times. So when our confusion boils over into a cancerous anxiety paralyzing us from doing anything because we are afraid we will mess God's plan up for our future relationship, this is a problem.

Theology Always Dictates Our Actions

A general truth seen throughout the Bible is that our inner beliefs dictate the way we feel and act in life. God has designed us to work from the inside out. Our inner man controls our outer lives. Therefore if you are anxious and paralyzed in your singleness this is really a theological issue.

For example, when David was a young man, he was shocked at Israel's passivity towards Goliath. David wondered to himself, "Why are all the men just standing around? What is everyone so afraid of?" I think we can ask ourselves those same questions when we look out over the sea of single

Christian men and women who are stuck doing nothing in fear of the unknowns that lie ahead in Christian dating and relationships.

I believe the reason David acted when he heard the threats of Goliath while all the other men were frozen in place was because of David's beliefs about God. Notice what Goliath was shouting to the Israelites day after day, "He stood and shouted to the ranks of Israel, 'Why have you come out to draw up for battle? Am I not a Philistine, and are you not servants of Saul?' . . . For forty days the Philistine came forward and took his stand, morning and evening" (1 Samuel 17:8, 16). When David saw what was happening he was so confused about how these men could allow this enemy to talk so blasphemous to God's army. Notice how David responds:

> "Then David said to the Philistine, 'You come to me with a sword and with a spear and with a javelin, but I come to you in the name of the Lord of hosts, the God of the armies of Israel, whom you have defied. [46] This day the Lord will deliver you into my hand, and I will strike you down and cut off your head.'" (1 Samuel 17:45-46)

The other men had swallowed Goliath's lie as he spewed them day after day, "You are servants of Saul!" Goliath disregarded Israel's God and said that Saul was their main leader. David disregarded this lie and proclaimed the truth, that he was a member of God's army. No other man corrected this theological mistake but David. It's really no surprise David was the only one with courage to act because

David was the only one with the right beliefs. Because David trusted in the power of "the Lord of hosts, the God of the armies of Israel" he was free to face what other men feared. Only when we trust God's sovereign power will we be free to act in faith. Notice too that in 1 Samuel 17:46-47 David trusted the sovereignty of God which allowed him to act:

> "This day the Lord will deliver you into my hand, and I will strike you down and cut off your head. And I will give the dead bodies of the host of the Philistines this day to the birds of the air and to the wild beasts of the earth, that all the earth may know that there is a God in Israel, [47] and that all this assembly may know that the Lord saves not with sword and spear. For the battle is the Lord's, and he will give you into our hand."

David knew God was in control of the future so this empowered him to act in faith during the present. David was confident that God had a plan for how this battle would end which empowered David to begin this battle without fear. I love that David proclaimed that he would cut off Goliath's head but he didn't even have a sword with him. This was not an accident, "and that all this assembly may know that the Lord saves not with sword and spear. For the battle is the Lord's, and he will give you into our hand" (1 Samuel 17:47). David was thinking about the glory of God, not the strength of Goliath. This is what gave David strength even when he faced an enormous obstacle.

He knew the victory was not in the sword he held but in the sovereignty of the God who held him. The Bible gives special emphasis to David's lack of a sword, "So David prevailed over the Philistine with a sling and with a stone, and struck the Philistine and killed him. There was no sword in the hand of David" (1 Samuel 17:50). The point is that victory comes by God. Imagine the scene: thousands of other older soldiers were standing on the sidelines in full battle attire, with swords on their hips but still passively dangling in their sheaths. David walked out even though he was less equipped because he knew if God willed him to beat Goliath, he would beat Goliath.

This does not mean we should start doing things without preparing. David had been trained through fighting bears and lions before facing Goliath (1 Samuel 17:34-36). The point here is not that we should just recklessly charge ahead in life and say, "Well, I know this seems foolish but God will provide." The point, rather, is that we will all need to move forward with God even when things are not perfect.

There are many roadblocks ahead if you desire to glorify God in your singleness, dating, and future marriage. But when you trust God you can begin moving forward even when you know things are not perfect. David didn't even have a sword, but that didn't stop him from trusting the sovereignty of God and heading onto the battle field. Throughout 1 Samuel 17:45-47 David's focus was not on what is but on what will be because of God's sovereignty. David knew God was in control and would deliver and accomplish the will God had for him. Therefore he acted in faith in 1 Samuel 17:48-54. His trust in God's sovereignty predated his heroic actions.

Likewise, if you hope to move forward in life, in relationships, and towards your future marriage, your trust in God must come before God moves on your behalf, not after. If you always wait to see God come through for you before you move forward, you will never move. God meets us in the moment. He asks us to step out in faith because he expects us to believe that he actually controls our future.

If You Fear Missing God's Will, You Are Probably Putting Too Much Faith in Man's Works Rather than in God's Grace

If you obey God's word you will not miss God's will.

Ironically the more you emphasize man's responsibility over God's sovereignty the more you become paralyzed to act because you feel it all depends on you. When you believe that if you make one wrong move you've blown it, you will not make very many moves unless you are ABSOLUTELY sure you are doing God's will. This is why people are often frozen and feel they cannot act in faith until they are certain they completely know what God wants them to do.

We should all be listening to hear the voice of God and seeking his counsel to direct our lives. But when you are desperate, frantic, and frozen in fear as you search for the clearest sign possible before you do anything, this is a sign you believe God is counting on you to accomplish his plan. If you are constantly waiting to do anything in relationships until you have an overabundance of confirmation, you probably fear that if you don't do the right thing you will miss God's grace.

When you know God is sovereign this frees you to act because you know God will guide your steps. People think incorrectly that if God is sovereign man should sit back and do nothing. But according to the Bible the opposite is true. When you believe God is sovereign this should empower you to live even more boldly because you know God is responsible for the results, not you. You must act, but God is going to do what God is going to do. When you think God is not involved, you end up being frozen because you think it all depends on you and you don't want to screw it up.

Ultimately this all comes down to a works-based theology versus a grace-based theology. When you have a works-based theology you believe that your actions are the defining variable in your salvation. This mentality carries over into the way you live every part of your life. You believe that your actions are not only the defining variable for your salvation but also the defining variable in how your singleness goes, how your dating pans out, who you marry, and what type of marriage you have.

But the Bible and real-life experience shows that you can do everything "just right" and still not get the results you think you should. You can be a mature Christian and do your best to marry just the right person, but you can still end up with a difficult marriage that is filled with issues and problems. You can't control who your spouse will become 10, 20, or 30 years into your marriage. The Bible obviously says there are consequences to our actions and we really do reap what we sow (Galatians 6:7-8), but it also does not say that life is one giant math problem and if you take the right steps you will get the exact results you want.

No, despite our actions God really does have a sovereign plan for each of our lives. When it comes to salvation, none of us did the right thing before we were saved. We didn't follow the right steps and then got saved because we found God's grace. The Bible says God had to reach out to us as we were in darkness. God called us before we could respond to him (John 6:44, Ephesians 2:4-5, Romans 5:8). By grace we have been saved, not by works.

While the initial shock of this can lead to confusion, when you embrace this and study what the Bible really says about God's sovereignty and grace, this is the foundation to a peaceful life. When you know that God, not you, is ultimately in control of your salvation and everything else in life, you will be empowered to live life without the fear of screwing everything up with just one wrong move. You can't lose your salvation because of something you might do. Why? Because you didn't get your salvation by anything you did. Likewise you are not the defining variable in God's will for your life. God is.

Yes, your actions matter and if you sin there are natural consequences to your poor decisions. God disciplines those he loves (Hebrews 12:6). You really do reap what you sow (Galatians 6:7-8). It's a problem, however, when you think that even when you are not sinning and you are doing your best to follow God that you will still somehow miss God's sovereign plan for your life. Because God is really in control, when you obey God it is impossible for you not to experience God's plan for your life. God will not let you miss his sovereign will when you obey his prescribed word.

Faith in God's Sovereignty Is the Secret to Being Empowered to Live Free and Overcome Fear

When you think God has a will for your relationships but God does not accomplish his will, you are creating the ingredients for a very long season of singleness. Ironically the result of an overemphasis on man's free will and an under emphasis on God's sovereign will has a slowing down process in people's dating approach. The more pressure they put on themselves to produce the right results, the more paralyzed they become to do anything because they are so afraid of screwing up.

When you believe God has a plan that you must figure out perfectly, follow perfectly, and only then will you accomplish the will of God for your life, you will be in a constant state of anxiety about your relationship status. But when you have a healthy balance between seeking to obey God's commands (prescribed will) and trusting God to fulfill his sovereign will, then you are able to live at peace as you actually live your life rather than waiting around for signs to completely confirm you are not blowing his will for your life.

Too much attention on the past produces depression. Too much attention on the future produces anxiety. Peace comes when we walk with God in the present. When worry is present this is a sign that you are emphasizing your works over God's sovereignty. Humans were created to be dependent. So much of this universe is outside of our control. When you start thinking that everything is in your control, you become anxious because you are taking on responsibilities you know you cannot handle or fulfill for yourself. Matthew 6:25-34 is a profound passage of Scripture in which Jesus teaches us the secret to living at peace:

> "Therefore I tell you, do not be anxious about your life, what you will eat or what you will drink, nor about your body, what you will put on. Is not life more than food, and the body more than clothing? [26] Look at the birds of the air: they neither sow nor reap nor gather into barns, and yet your heavenly Father feeds them. Are you not of more value than they? [27] And which of you by being anxious can add a single hour to his span of life? [28] And why are you anxious about clothing? Consider the lilies of the field, how they grow: they neither toil nor spin, [29] yet I tell you, even Solomon in all his glory was not arrayed like one of these. [30] But if God so clothes the grass of the field, which today is alive and tomorrow is thrown into the oven, will he not much more clothe you, O you of little faith? [31] Therefore do not be anxious, saying, 'What shall we eat?' or 'What shall we drink?' or 'What shall we wear?' [32] For the Gentiles seek after all these things, and your heavenly Father knows that you need them all. [33] But seek first the kingdom of God and his righteousness, and all these things will be added to you. [34] Therefore do not be anxious about tomorrow, for tomorrow will be anxious for itself. Sufficient for the day is its own trouble."

Jesus is not condemning the questions about food, drink, or clothing. He is condemning the anxiety underneath these questions that are rooted in a lack of faith in God's goodness. Jesus is condemning the false belief that you can actually produce good for yourself and add days to your life. The only thing you can produce without God is worry.

Notice the solution Jesus gives for the anxiety about the unknowns in the future, "Therefore do not be anxious, saying, 'What shall we eat?' or 'What shall we drink?' or 'What shall we wear?' For the Gentiles seek after all these things, and your heavenly Father knows that you need them all" (Matthew 6:31-32).

"Your heavenly Father knows that you need them all." In other words, God has a plan. Anxiety about the future is a symptom of a lack of faith in God's ability to provide you with what you need. When you believe in the sovereignty of God, you are not called to just sit around and wait for manna from heaven. Jesus was not saying don't work and act to get the food, drink, and clothing that you need. He was saying that you should not be anxious because God will provide if you obey him. Notice Jesus says God will provide but then he gives us all a command of action, "But seek first the kingdom of God and his righteousness, and all these things will be added to you" (Matthew 6:33).

These principles apply perfectly to your hope for a future marriage. It's not wrong to ask the questions. It's not wrong to wonder how God will provide you with a spouse one day. You absolutely should seek to hear the voice of God and follow his plan for your life. It's wrong, however, when you doubt God's ability to accomplish his plan and therefore you are filled with anxiety.

When you put God first and simply seek to please God in every aspect of your life, God will not let you miss his will for your life.

I can't promise you anything about your future other than that God is in control. Trust him. He is worthy.

Reflection Questions:

1. Why was David able to face the enemy when all the other men were being passive? How can this relate to the current trends in Christian dating?

2. Why was it significant that David faced Goliath without a sword? What does this teach you about accomplishing God's will for your life?

3. What impact does a "works based theology" have on your dating approach and your interactions with the opposite sex? In other words, how do you feel when you think everything depends on you rather than on God?

4. How should we respond to the truth of God's sovereignty? Should this cause us to do less or more? Explain.

5. Read Matthew 6:33. What do you learn from this verse?

Thank You!

Thank you for reading this book! I truly pray God used it to help you trust his sovereign will for your singleness, dating, and future marriage.

If you enjoyed this book and found it useful, would you consider leaving a review on Amazon? No pressure! The only reason I ask is because the more reviews a book receives the more likely other people will read it too. I hope many can learn to trust God's sovereign plan for their future marriages. By leaving a review on Amazon you are helping accomplish that goal with me!

Lastly, I would love for you to stay in touch with me by connecting with me on ApplyGodsWord.com, YouTube, and on all my other social media channels. I have a lot of other books you may enjoy too which you can find on ApplyGodsWord.com or on Amazon.

If you join my email list, you will never miss anything new I put out and you will gain instant access to all my free eBooks. Just visit the website and you will see how to submit your email to the list. Thousands of other have already become AGW subscribers. It's totally free and you can remove your email from this list at anytime, so there's really nothing to lose!

God bless!
-Mark

Contact us at:
Website: ApplyGodsWord.com
YouTube: www.youtube.com/c/ApplyGodsWordcomMarkBallenger
Twitter: @Apply_GodsWord
Facebook: www.facebook.com/ApplyGodsWord/
Email: markballenger@applygodsword.com

Appendix

How to Know If God Is Calling You to Singleness

Perhaps one of the most prevalent questions amongst single Christians is, "How will I know if God wants me to get married or remain single?" Marriage is a big deal to God. Marriage is central to reflecting the gospel (Ephesians 5:22-33), it is the way God has ordained the human race to be populated (Genesis 1:28), and thus most Christians are called to be married. There are many Christians, however, who are called to singleness. So how will you know if God is calling you to singleness?

You May Be Called By God to Singleness If You Know Your Whole Focus Should Be on Ministry

Often times the problem is that the church you attend values marriage or singleness more than the other. The Bible makes clear, however, that both marriage and singleness are equally important callings from God. 1 Corinthians 7:38 states, "So then he who marries his betrothed does well, and he who refrains from marriage will do even better."

At first glance, 1 Corinthians 7:38 seems to totally disprove my statement that marriage and singleness are equally important callings from God. Notice, though, that this verse begins with "So." Paul says that those who choose the calling of singleness "do even better" because in 1 Corinthians 7:29-35, Paul explains that the value of singleness is that you can focus solely on God. He goes as far to say, "From now on, let those who have wives live as though they had none" (1 Corinthians 7:29).

Clearly Paul is not saying that husbands should abandon their wives and families to serve the Lord. The point of this passage is that whether you are married or single, your goal should be to serve the Lord with the same focus as someone who is single because they have committed their life to serving the Lord. This is why he said in 1 Corinthians 7:38 that those who choose Christian singleness have done better.

It's not better to be single than it is to be married. It is better, however, that you seek to serve the Lord and not have other distractions. But to deny your calling of marriage would be to dishonor the Lord. If you are called to marriage, you must seek to serve the Lord with the same passion that you would have if you were a Christian called to singleness. Paul qualified his statements when he declared, "I wish that all were as I myself am [single]. But each has his own gift from God, one of one kind and one of another" (1 Corinthians 7:7).

With all that said, one way you will know if God is calling you to singleness is if your motivation is simply to serve the Lord. If you have a desire to live a Christian life of singleness because you hate men, don't want to submit to a husband, don't want the responsibility of caring for a wife, don't want to deal with all the emotional wounds you experienced because of your parents failed marriage, don't want to stop dating multiple people – if your desire to remain single is anything other than to please the Lord, this is not a sign that you are called to singleness.

If You Don't "burn with passion"/Sexual Desires, God May Be Calling You to Singleness

"Does God want me to be single forever?" One sign that will help you determine if God wants you to be single is if he completely takes away your sexual desires. Again, it is crucial to make sure your feelings and desires are not rooted in unhealthy wounds. For example, if you don't have a sexual desire because you were sexually abused as a child, this is not a sign you are called to singleness.

If, however, you are seeking to love God and deal with the wounds of your past but you simply don't have a strong sexual drive, this may be a sign that God wants you to be single forever. God does not want you to be single if you burn with sexual passion. 1 Corinthians 7:1-2, 8-9 explains:

> "Now concerning the matters about which you wrote: "It is good for a man not to have sexual relations with a woman." [2] But because of the temptation to sexual immorality, each man should have his own wife and each woman her own husband. . . . To the unmarried and the widows I say that it is good for them to remain single as I am. [9] But if they cannot exercise self-control, they should marry. For it is better to marry than to burn with passion."

None of this means that just because you have a sexual desire it is a guarantee you will one day be married. God's ways and plans for us are sometimes not that clear. God knows what he's doing, but he doesn't always reveal everything so clearly to us when we want to know. If you do have a sexual desire, however, this is good biblical evidence that you should pursue marriage.

Religious Reasons Will Not Help You Know If God Is Calling You to Christian Singleness

Marriage is a gift from God. Marriage should never disqualify anyone from any type of godly ministry. Sadly, there are many religions today that claim celibacy and singleness are requirements for holiness. 1 Timothy 4:1-5 explains:

> "Now the Spirit expressly says that in later times some will depart from the faith by devoting themselves to deceitful spirits and teachings of demons, [2] through the insincerity of liars whose consciences are seared, [3] who forbid marriage and require abstinence from foods that God created to be received with thanksgiving by those who believe and know the truth. [4] For everything created by God is good, and nothing is to be rejected if it is received with thanksgiving, [5] for it is made holy by the word of God and prayer."

If you want to serve the Lord, this is not a sign that you are called by God to singleness. God can call you to marriage or singleness and call you to serve him in full-time ministry as well. While many Christian religions like Catholicism certainly do many good things for God's kingdom, their teaching on priestly celibacy is simply unbiblical.

Love God and He Will Reveal His Calling for You, Whether It's Marriage or Christian Singleness

You may not be able to know if God wants you to stay single forever. Most of the time God does not give us signs that would reveal his whole plan for our life all at once. Rather than spend your whole life seeking signs on whether or not God has called you to marriage or singleness, the wiser approach is to do what you know God has called you to do.

We all know God has called all Christians to love him and other people. When we simply seek the Lord with all of our heart, God will reveal the next part of his calling for us when we need to know it. There are certainly some biblical ways to know whether or not God is calling you to singleness; ultimately, though, each Christian will simply need to seek the Lord and obey what he or she feels led to do.

Marriage and singleness are both wonderful callings from God. If you desire to be married and not remain single forever, odds are God has not called you to singleness. Only God truly knows what his plan for you is, so seek the Lord and in due time he will make it all clear.

God may want you to be single or he may want you to be married, but you do know he definitely wants you to serve and love him right now.

Is Singleness Better than Marriage?

Does the Bible say singleness is better than marriage? When you read through 1 Corinthians 7, at first glance this seems like an easy question to answer. Yes, singleness is better than marriage. For example 1 Corinthians 7:38 states, "So then he who marries his betrothed does well, and he who refrains from marriage will do even better."

However, to just say, "Yes, singleness is better than marriage," would be an oversimplification of what 1 Corinthians actually says. The context of each verse in 1 Corinthians 7 is crucial. If you pull one verse out, like 1 Corinthians 7:38, it will seem like singleness is better. But if you pull out just one other verse, like 1 Corinthians 7:2, you can make it seem like everyone should be married, "But because of the temptation to sexual immorality, each man should have his own wife and each woman her own husband."

The key is to keep each verse in context and factor in all the variables that 1 Corinthians 7 discusses when trying to answer, "Does the Bible say singleness is better than marriage?"

Singleness Is Better Than Marriage In General, Not Specifically For Individuals

The main point I hope to prove in this article is that 1 Corinthians 7 isn't prescribing singleness or marriage but rather telling Christians to make the choices that help each of us most glorify God. Each individual is made different by God, thus singleness may be better for some and marriage may be better for some. Glorifying God, however, is the main point.

When you take individual needs out of the equation and you simply look at marriage and singleness in principle, singleness is better. Again, this does not mean singleness is automatically better for every person, but when you subtract the individual factors that come into play with real people, singleness is better than marriage in general. 1 Corinthians 7:32-35, 38 states this truth:

> "I want you to be free from anxieties. The unmarried man is anxious about the things of the Lord, how to please the Lord. [33] But the married man is anxious about worldly things, how to please his wife, [34] and his interests are divided. And the unmarried or betrothed woman is anxious about the things of the Lord, how to be holy in body and spirit. But the married woman is anxious about worldly things, how to please her husband. [35] I say this for your own benefit, not to lay any restraint upon you, but to promote good order and to secure your undivided devotion to the Lord. . . . So then he who marries his betrothed does well, and he who refrains from marriage will do even better."

When people argue that singleness is better than marriage, these Bible verses are what they refer to. Clearly after reading these verses it is plain that singleness is better than marriage. I don't know how else to interpret what Paul said.

However, Paul, again, is speaking about marriage and singleness in general without a specific person in the equation. Paul was not talking to Sammie, Jane, or Carlos. Singleness is better than marriage in that singleness eliminates other responsibilities which can distract people from serving God. But we can't end here. We now have to talk about marriage and singleness on the individual level because that's what Paul does in 1 Corinthians 7.

Singleness Is Not Better Than Marriage On an Individual Bases

Paul never said singleness is better for everyone. His point was that singleness is better than marriage in general. If singleness was always better for every individual human, God would command every individual human to be single. For example, 1 Corinthians 7:8-9 states:

> "To the unmarried and the widows I say that it is good for them to remain single, as I am. ^{9} But if they cannot exercise self-control, they should marry. For it is better to marry than to burn with passion."

Now Paul said, "it is better to marry." But why did he say that? He said that because there are now other factors in the equation. Singleness is better than marriage when no individual factors come into play. But when there are individual factors in the equation, marriage may be better than singleness for that individual.

For example, as we just read in 1 Corinthians 7:8-9, one sign that you are called to singleness is that you do not have a sexual desire. If you do have a strong sexual desire this is a sign that you should pursue marriage. In John Piper's article titled, *Married or Single: For Better or Worse?* he explains:

> "The "compelling" comes only from the right combination of internal realities and objective truths about God's design for marriage. When the right combination is not there, marriage is not compelling

> and should not be. I would say the same thing about singleness.
>
> There is more to marriage and singleness than I have mentioned. But the point is to show that neither I nor the Bible is saying that either is compelling in and of themselves. That is why Paul says, "One has one gift and one another" (1 Corinthians 7:7). I think he means: The internal reality of one person finds one of these powerfully compelling and the internal reality of another finds another powerfully compelling. And I would add: This can change from one season to another."

As Piper notes, what is better for someone may change over time. Singleness may be better for you when you are in your early 20s because God has placed a desire on your heart to serve in the army. But perhaps when you get out of the army you really want to serve God by loving a wife and a family. Then marriage would be better for you. The examples are endless here. The point is that seasons of life bring in different factors that affect whether singleness or marriage is better for an individual.

Singleness and Marriage Are Not the Main Point of 1 Corinthians 7. Serving God Is the Point

In short, singleness is better for you if you have the gift of singleness. Marriage is better for you if you have the gift of marriage. But all gifts from God have a specific purpose. They are to be used to serve and glorify God.

The main point I hope I have made in this article is that 1 Corinthians 7 isn't prescribing singleness or marriage but rather telling Christians to make the choices that help each of us most glorify God. The common command for all Christians is to do whatever you need to do to obey and honor God, whether that is singleness or marriage. Singleness and marriage are not pleasing or displeasing in and of themselves. Rather, Paul's point in 1 Corinthians 7 is that singleness and marriage are tools that we must use to serve God. Which tool you need will be based upon what needs you have. A shovel is not better than a hammer unless you need a shovel to accomplish your tasks. 1 Corinthians 7:29-31, 35 states:

> "This is what I mean, brothers: the appointed time has grown very short. From now on, let those who have wives live as though they had none, [30] and those who mourn as though they were not mourning, and those who rejoice as though they were not rejoicing, and those who buy as though they had no goods, [31] and those who deal with the world as though they had no dealings with it. For the present form of this world is passing away. . . . I say this for your own benefit, not to lay any restraint upon you, but to promote good order and to secure your undivided devotion to the Lord."

Paul says a lot in 1 Corinthians 7, but here we have the main point. He just told married people to live as though they are unmarried. Obviously this does not mean we should neglect our spouses because this would directly contradict 1 Corinthians 7:5, "Do not deprive one another, except perhaps by agreement for a limited time, that you may devote yourselves to prayer; but then come together again, so that Satan may not tempt you because of your lack of self-control."

Paul's point is that those who are married should live as though they are single in that they focus on the Lord with all their heart. All Christians should take the general benefits of singleness that make it better than marriage and live to please Christ in all things. Paul says:

> "From now on, let those who have wives live as though they had none, [30] and those who mourn as though they were not mourning, and those who rejoice as though they were not rejoicing, and those who buy as though they had no goods, [31] and those who deal with the world as though they had no dealings with it."

Rejoicing, mourning, buying goods, or not buying goods is not the main point of 1 Corinthians 7 just as singleness and marriage are not the main point of 1 Corinthians 7. The main point is that we all should serve God to our greatest ability, "I say this for your own benefit, not to lay any restraint upon you, but to promote good order and to secure your undivided devotion to the Lord" (1 Corinthians 7:35). In John MacArthur's article titled *Is Singleness Better than Marriage?* he states:

> "Although celibacy is good for Christians who are not married, it is a gift from God that He does not give to every believer. Just as it is wrong to misuse a gift that we have, it is also wrong to try to use a gift we do not have. For a person who does not have the gift of celibacy, trying to practice it brings moral and spiritual frustration. But for those who have it as God's gift, singleness, like all His gifts, is a great blessing."

Jesus told the disciples on one occasion, "Not all men can accept this statement, but only those to whom it has been given. For there are eunuchs who were born that way from their mother's womb; and there are eunuchs who were made eunuchs by men; and there are also eunuchs who made themselves eunuchs for the sake of the kingdom of heaven. He who is able to accept this, let him accept it" (Matt. 19:12).

Both Jesus and Paul make it clear that the celibate life is not required by God for all believers and that it can be lived satisfactorily only by those to whom God has given it.

Is Singleness Better than Marriage According to the Bible?

So the Bible does say singleness is better than marriage, but it does not say singleness is better than marriage for every individual. When certain factors are at play, marriage is better. If you have the gift of singleness, singleness is better for you. If you have the gift of marriage, then marriage is better for you. What is best for every Christian is that we use the gifts God has given us for his glory.

How to Be Saved By Jesus

To be saved by Jesus, you have to first admit you need to be saved. But saved from what? Sin. What is sin? Sin is our willful disobedience towards God. Romans 3:23 states, "for all have sinned and fall short of the glory of God." Every single human (other than Jesus) who has ever walked this planet, including you and me, have sinned against God.

The Bible says that because we have sinned we cannot have fellowship with God and we will eventually reap what we sow if we do not turn to Jesus. Romans 6:23 explains, "For the wages of sin is death, but the free gift of God is eternal life in Christ Jesus our Lord." Sin causes spiritual, emotional, relational, economic, social, environmental, and even physical death. Everything bad and evil is because the human race has fallen and we now live in a broken world.

Sin has separated us from God. But God loves us so much, he made a way for our relationship with him to be completely restored. Jesus is the way, for he said, "I am the way and the truth and the life. No one comes to the Father except through me" (John 14:6).

Jesus took the death we deserved. He took our place so we could escape the punishment that belonged to us.

Put Your Faith In Jesus, Confess, and Repent Of Sin To Be Saved

Although the wages of sin are death, God offers us all the free gift of eternal life through Jesus Christ our Lord. None of us deserve this gift, but God offers it to us because he loves us, "but God shows his love for us in that while we were still sinners, Christ died for us" (Romans 5:8).

But how do we receive this gift? The Bible says that although Jesus paid for your sins, you still must put your faith in Jesus to receive his grace. If you choose not to believe in Jesus, you cannot receive God's gift of salvation through Jesus Christ.

Here are thee important points regarding salvation.

The first is faith in Jesus: "For by grace you have been saved through faith. And this is not your own doing; it is the gift of God, [9] not a result of works, so that no one may boast" (Ephesians 2:8-9). Putting your faith in Jesus means you believe he died on the cross for your sins, he rose from the grave, and you now know you can never save yourself through works but only through believing in Jesus.

The second is confessing your sins: "If we say we have no sin, we deceive ourselves, and the truth is not in us. [9] If we confess our sins, he is faithful and just to forgive us our sins and to cleanse us from all unrighteousness" (1 John 1:8-9). To be forgiven by God, all we need to do is confess our sins and he will wipe us clean with the blood of Jesus.

The third is repentance of your sin: "Repent and be baptized, every one of you, in the name of Jesus Christ for the forgiveness of your sins. And you will receive the gift of the Holy Spirit" (Acts 2:38). Repentance is the next step after confession. Confessing is asking forgiveness. Repentance is about turning your life away from sin and running back to God. Repentance is about living for God.

You are saved by grace, through faith, and for good works done unto God (Ephesians 2:8-10).

Are You Ready To Be Saved By Jesus Christ?

If you are ready to be saved, then put your faith in Jesus, ask God to forgive you of your sins, repent by turning from your old life, and now seek to live for God in obedience to him. There is a lot more to learn, but your journey with God begins here.

There's no magical prayer that will save you, but praying these words are a way of doing what we've talked about in this section. Pray this prayer in faith if you want to become a Christian and have a personal relationship with God.

Dear God,
I believe Jesus Christ came to earth, died on the cross for my sins, and rose from the grave. I put my faith in Jesus. I confess all my sins to you and ask for your forgiveness. And I pray that you would help me to repent of my old life. Help me to follow you now. Thank you for saving me. In Jesus name, Amen.

If you've just now become a Christian, please email me and let me know (markballenger@applygodsword.com). I would love to celebrate with you and send you some helpful resources!

God bless,
Mark

Made in the USA
Lexington, KY
13 April 2019